STUDY GUIDE FOR *LET NOBODY TURN US AROUND*

Second Edition

KAREN G. WILLIAMS
ANDREA QUEELEY

ROWMAN & LITTLEFIELD PUBLISHERS, INC.
Lanham • Boulder • New York • Toronto • Plymouth, UK

ROWMAN & LITTLEFIELD PUBLISHERS, INC.

Published in the United States of America by Rowman & Littlefield Publishers, Inc. A Member of the Rowman & Littlefield Publishing Group, 4501 Forbes Boulevard, Suite 200, Lanham, Maryland 20706, www.rowmanlittlefield.com

Estover Road
Plymouth PL6 7PY
United Kingdom

British Library Cataloguing in Publication Information Available

Library of Congress Cataloging-in-Publication Data

Williams, Karen G.
Study guide for let nobody turn us around / Karen G. Williams and Andrea Queeley. — 2nd ed.
p. cm.
ISBN 978-1-4422-0013-5 (pbk. : alk. paper) — ISBN 978-1-4422-0014-2 (electronic)
1. Let nobody turn us around—Examinations—Study guides. 2. African Americans—History—Examinations—Study guides. 3. African Americans—Civil rights—History—Examinations—Study guides. 4. African Americans—Social conditions—Examinations—Study guides. I. Queeley, Andrea. II. Title.
E184.6.L4837 2009
973'.0496073—dc22 2009019697

Printed in the United States of America

∞™ The paper used in this publication meets the minimum requirements of American National Standard for Information Sciences—Permanence of Paper for Printed Library Materials, ANSI/NISO Z39.48-1992.

STUDY GUIDE FOR *LET NOBODY TURN US AROUND*

CONTENTS

INTRODUCTION TO THE STUDY GUIDE

Let Nobody Turn Us Around: Voices of Resistance, Reform, and Renewal provides students with a collection of readings that capture the main ideological currents of the Black Freedom movement in the United States from 1768 to the present. Each section begins with an introductory essay to frame the ideas and activism of the period under consideration. Although each document contains a preface that situates the text and its author in the context of the political activism of the time, the documents themselves are meant to inform readers about the theoretical underpinnings of the activism rather than the particular movements themselves.

This study guide is designed to complement each section of the book. Key Points, summaries of the section introductions, highlight the main points and thus offer guidance for lecture preparation. Following these summaries, Comprehension and Thought Questions address each individual document appearing in the section. These questions range in difficulty and are aimed at ensuring that the student recognizes key factual aspects of the document or its author; the questions address the significant ideas and features. They can be answered without the use of outside sources and many require that the student reflect upon her own experiences or opinions.

Essay Questions that address major themes are provided for the introduction and each of the five sections. Ideal for use in exams or homework assignments, these questions require the student to draw upon several readings in the section, incorporate the information presented, and use it to form a coherent response. Though students can utilize substantiated knowledge from outside of the text, the documents should be the basis upon which students' responses are formulated. The Essay Questions provide instructors with an opportunity to assess student reading comprehension as well as analytical skills. Some of the questions might also form the basis for classroom discussion.

Suggested Research Topics follow the Essay Questions; these are derived from the themes and issues of the section. The topics suggest areas of investigation that would be ideal for more comprehensive student projects requiring considerable outside research. The items are meant to be fairly general, to allow the student to choose an aspect of the topic that he wishes to research in depth, exercising creativity and motivation. The Classroom Exercises suggest activities aimed at fostering student engagement with the subject through interaction with the instructor and other students. Instructors are encouraged to tailor these exercises to fit the needs of their particular classroom environment.

The final feature of the study guide, Media and Internet Resources, is a list of films and websites that are relevant to each section. The films are ideal for classroom viewing and discussion. The websites provide an additional teaching and learning tool for teachers and students who wish to enhance their understanding of the themes and topics presented in *Let Nobody Turn Us Around.*

INTRODUCTION

Resistance, Reform, and Renewal in the Black Experience

KEY POINTS

1. **African Americans' historical depth**. Africans brought to and enslaved in North America came with individual and group histories. The authors emphasize the agency of African Americans both within the institution of slavery and after its demise by pointing to their struggle for equality.
2. **Integrationism and black nationalism**. These two opposing ideologies emerged during the debate over the abolition of slavery. A third perspective that emerged from labor activism is identified as **transformationism**. Though the roots of transformationism extend back into the nineteenth century (exemplified by figures such as Nat Turner and Henry Highland Garnett, who sought to dismantle structures of oppression), Black radicalism as an ideological position solidified with the development of the Black working class in the twentieth century.
3. **Race, class, and gender**. These issues have been central to theorizing African-American liberation. Black women activists have been at the forefront of this conceptualization.
4. **Theory**. This book's emphasis is on the theory that has informed social movements rather than on the movements themselves. Students

are encouraged to connect the theoretical claims put forth in the works in this volume to social movements.

ESSAY QUESTIONS

1. What do you think are the strengths and weaknesses of integrationism, black nationalism, and transformationalism?
2. Identify at least three organizations or public figures that subscribe to each ideology (nine total). Organizations and figures can be from the past or contemporary period. Briefly explain why you think that they adhere to an integrationist, black nationalist, or transformationalist ideology.
3. Why do you think that race, class, and gender have been central to theorizing African-American liberation and that black women have been leaders in this way of theorizing?

CLASSROOM EXERCISES

1. Divide the classroom into two teams and have a formal debate with each team representing an opposing ideology.
2. Have students write answers to the following questions and share their responses with the class: How do race, gender, and class affect people's lives? How have these issues affected your life?

SECTION ONE

FOUNDATIONS

Slavery and Abolitionism, 1768–1861

KEY POINTS

- **Racism historically constructed.** The belief in the innate inferiority of people of African descent was developed and accepted over time in the context of chattel slavery. This suggests that racism is a historically constructed social phenomenon rather than a biological—and therefore natural—occurrence between inherently inferior and superior groups.
- **Resistance.** Different groups of people of African descent resisted the institution of slavery by various means. Resistance is overt collective action designed for an immediate end to a specific form of repression.
- **Reform.** There were also different strategies of reform. One strategy was to enlist the assistance of white sympathizers and another was to link the anti-slavery movement to other struggles of the time. Reform is long-term gradual change based on dialogue and reconciliation.
- **Renewal.** The renewal of communities came through the affirmation of bonds of family, community, and humanity. It refers to the efforts by a group (such as fostering institutions to provide goods and services) to ensure its own survival and sustainability. The church was the most important institution in this process.
- **Solidarity.** The creation of a "black world" of social institutions was based on the appeal to racial solidarity and collective self-help. This

could not have been achieved without a belief in the existence of a global kinship among people of African descent and in the interconnectedness of their fate.

COMPREHENSION AND THOUGHT QUESTIONS

1. "On Being Brought from Africa to America," *Phillis Wheatley, 1768*
   a. What was Wheatley's first publication? How did Wheatley secure this publication?
   b. What is the overall message that Wheatley is communicating?
   c. Why do you think Wheatley used the word "sable" instead of "black" or "dark" or another descriptive word to describe her race? What connotations does "sable" invoke?
   d. Who do you think Wheatley is referring to when she writes, "Their colour is a diabolic die"? Why do you think that Wheatley adds quotation marks to this line? Do you think Wheatley meant "dye" instead of "die"? Why or why not?
2. "The Interesting Narrative of the Life of Olaudah Equiano," *Olaudah Equiano, 1789*
   a. In what century did Olaudah Equiano live?
   b. How old was he when he was sold into slavery?
   c. Name three things that he experienced during the Middle Passage.
   d. What was the first place in the Americas that he landed?
   e. In Equiano's narrative, he mentions slavery being a part of life in his homeland of eastern Nigeria. Do you think the experiences of slavery in Africa differed from those in the Americas? How and why?
3. "Thus Doth Ethiopia Stretch Forth Her Hand from Slavery . . . ," *Prince Hall, 1797*
   a. What organization did Prince Hall help to initiate?
   b. In what other movement was he involved?
   c. Hall makes reference to conditions in the West Indies. How do you think he was informed of slavery in other parts of the Americas and what was the importance of knowing about what was happening outside of North America?

4. The Founding of the African Methodist Episcopal Church, *Richard Allen, 1816*
    a. What social institution did Richard Allen help to found?
    b. What incident led Allen to found this institution?
    c. How does the exclusion of African Americans from European American religious institutions relate to the integrationism vs. black nationalism debate?
5. David Walker's "Appeal," *1829–1830*
    a. To what African-American newspaper did David Walker contribute?
    b. What kind of tactics did he encourage enslaved African Americans to employ in order to achieve liberation?
    c. On what does David Walker blame the suffering of people of African descent?
    d. What are the hypocrisies that Walker points to in this appeal? Why do you think that he points out such contradictions?
    e. Throughout his narrative, Walker uses innumerable explanations and appears to be very agitated. Why is David Walker so angry?
6. The Statement of Nat Turner, *1831*
    a. How many years before the outbreak of the Civil War did Nat Turner lead a slave revolt?
    b. How many people participated in this rebellion?
    c. Who wrote Turner's confessions?
    d. Why did people say that Nat Turner would be a prophet?
    e. Why did Nat Turner return to the plantation that he had run away from?
    f. In this document, Turner is recorded as receiving spiritual guidance throughout his life. How is the relationship between resistance and spirituality evidenced in his story? What do you think about the relationship between religion or spirituality and social change?
    g. What were the specific reasons Turner gives for his revolt?
    h. When the interviewer asks Turner if he is sorry for his violent actions, how does he respond?
7. Slaves Are Prohibited to Read and Write by Law
    a. What were the punishments for educating a slave?

b. The punishment for teaching a slave to read, write, and perform mathematical calculations is different for a white person, a free "colored" person, and a slave. What do the differences tell you about the social structure of slave society?
c. Why were slave owners so concerned about slaves being educated?

8. "What If I Am a Woman?" *Maria W. Stewart, 1833*
   a. To what areas of social activism were women limited?
   b. According to Stewart, what would allow the man of color to be as successful as white men?
   c. What does she implore people to do in order to improve their condition?
   d. By calling for heightened moral standards in the black community, is Stewart laying the responsibility for the black condition on black people themselves? Explain.
9. A Slave Denied the Rights to Marry, *Letter of Milo Thompson, Slave, 1834*
   a. From reading this document, what attitude did white slaveholders appear to have about their slaves getting married?
   b. Do you think slaveholding whites viewed blacks primarily as their property, as human beings, or as both? Explain.
   c. What were the consequences of the slaveholders' attitudes and practices about slave marriages on the enslaved?
   d. What impact do you think that the form of coercion described in this section had on individuals and communities?
10. The Selling of Slaves, *Advertisement, 1835*
    a. When was the transatlantic slave trade technically outlawed?
    b. What was the legal status of a slave?
    c. What could slaves be exchanged for?
    d. What elements of the descriptions of enslaved people in the advertisements strike you? What do they reveal about the African-American population?
11. Solomon Northrup Describes a New Orleans Slave Auction, *1841*
    a. How did Solomon Northrup become a slave?
    b. What was the name of his narrative?
    c. What would hurt the sale of a slave?

   d. How do you think the auction block experience described in this section impacted African Americans? How did reading this impact you?
12. Cinque and the *Amistad* Revolt, *1841*
   a. Where was the ship *Amistad* headed at the time of the revolt?
   b. Where in the United States did *Amistad* land?
   c. On what basis did the Supreme Court rule to free the Africans of *Amistad*?
   d. What does this case reveal about the difference between a "kidnapped African" and a slave?
13. "Let Your Motto Be Resistance!" *Henry Highland Garnett, 1843*
   a. By what means did Henry Highland Garnett advocate for the overthrow of the system of slavery?
   b. What president did Garnett advise?
   c. What was his alternative to seeking racial justice in the United States?
   d. Where did Garnett die?
   e. Why do you think that Garnett talked about the American Revolution in this argument for the overthrow of slavery?
   f. How did Garnett's religious beliefs influence his argument against slavery?
14. "Slavery as It Is," *William Wells Brown, 1847*
   a. How many times did William Wells Brown try to escape slavery?
   b. In what social reform movements was he a leader?
   c. Name three of Brown's works.
   d. What do you think was the effect of discussing how Europeans have responded to the contradiction between American slavery and democracy?
15. "A'n't I a Woman?" *Sojourner Truth, 1851*
   a. Sojourner Truth is considered to be the foremother of what ideology?
   b. How did Truth come to be free?
   c. From the two versions of Truth's speech, identify her arguments for the rights of women and African Americans. Why do you think that she didn't contest the idea that women and black people had less "intellect" than white men?

d. How did "Sojourner" acquire her name and what did her name signify?
e. How do you think an audience of white women felt about Sojourner Truth's arguments about women and gender?
f. What did the phrase "A'n't I a Woman?" convey to white women sitting in the audience listening to Sojourner Truth?

16. "A Plea for Emigration, or Notes of Canada West," *Mary Ann Shadd Cary, 1852*
    a. Mary Ann Shadd Cary was the first African-American woman to achieve what?
    b. Why did Shadd Cary write this pamphlet?
    c. If most African Americans were enslaved and could not read or write, who do you think was her intended audience?
    d. What is the "aristocracy of birth" that Shadd Cary describes?
    e. How does Shadd Cary describe Canada and Canadians?
17. A Black Nationalist Manifesto, *Martin R. Delany, 1852*
    a. Of what political ideology was Martin R. Delany a major architect?
    b. Over what did he and Frederick Douglass differ?
    c. What did Delany advocate in order to elevate people of color?
    d. What does this document reveal about the role of gender in the oppression and liberation of African Americans, according to Delany?
    e. Did Delany believe that black people have a future in the United States? Why or why not?
    f. What are the advantages for African Americans who emigrate to Central, South America, and West Indies?
18. "What to the Slave Is the Fourth of July?" *Frederick Douglass, 1852*
    a. Why do you think that white abolitionists invited Frederick Douglass to speak at the Fourth of July celebration?
    b. Douglass describes the celebration of the Fourth of July and, by implication, American democracy as hypocritical. What reasons does he give for his criticism of American political institutions?
    c. Why did Douglass write the *Narrative of the Life of Frederick Douglass*?
    d. In what reform movements was Douglass involved?
    e. Where did Douglass live outside of the United States?

f. Does Douglass reject American democracy or does he want to be included within it? Explain your answer using the text.
g. Do you think that Douglass's arguments against the celebration of the Fourth of July are relevant in contemporary U.S. society? Why or why not?

19. "No Rights That a White Man Is Bound to Respect": The Dred Scott Case and Its Aftermath
    a. Who was Dred Scott?
    b. On what basis did Scott win his suit? On what basis was this victory overruled?
    c. What is the role of race in the court's decision to deny Dred Scott his freedom?
    d. Why did Chief Justice Taney state that the Negro has "no rights that the white man is bound to respect"?
20. "Whenever the Colored Man Is Elevated . . . ," *John S. Rock, 1858*
    a. John Rock was the first African American to do what?
    b. Against what claim about the Black man does Rock argue?
    c. Why do you think that Rock incorporates a comparison of white and black physical appearance in his speech?
21. The Spirituals: "Go Down, Moses" and "Didn't My Lord Deliver Daniel"
    a. What roles did spirituals play in the lives of the enslaved?
    b. Do you think that Christianity was a positive or negative force in the lives of African Americans during slavery? Why or why not?
    c. Based on the lyrics of the spirituals, what differences seem to exist between white Christianity and religion in the enslaved community?
    d. Many spirituals emphasize images from the Old Testament, especially the story of Exodus. Why did the Exodus story have an impact upon African Americans?

ESSAY QUESTIONS

1. How are the themes of resistance, reform, and renewal evidenced in this section? Draw examples from at least ten of the twenty-one excerpts.

2. The authors state in the introduction that slave narratives were a mechanism by which whites were swayed to sympathize with the abolition movement. What parts in Olaudah Equiano's narrative would encourage late-eighteenth-century European Americans to join the movement and why?
3. Based on the excerpts in this section, describe the day-to-day experience of slavery. How was this experience different for men and women, people born in Africa and those born in America, and children and adults?
4. Identify evidence of the relationship between the anti-slavery movement and religion. What role did religion play in African Americans' struggle to end slavery?
5. Compare and contrast the cases of Dred Scott and *Amistad*. What do these cases reveal about race, nationality, and the U.S. legal system?
6. Drawing from the commentary in this section, identify and explain the grounds upon which African Americans argued for the destruction of the institution of slavery.
7. Using the documents written by women, discuss the breadth of the themes covered. What do these women writers reveal about the predicament for women and for African Americans during this time?

SUGGESTED RESEARCH TOPICS

1. The lives, work, and activism of free African Americans in the eighteenth and nineteenth centuries
2. The church in the African-American community
3. The historical trajectory of the Back-to-Africa movement
4. Slave resistance in the Americas
5. Black women and social activism
6. The immigration of African Americans to places outside the United States during the eighteenth and nineteenth centuries
7. Eighteenth- and nineteenth-century poetry, fiction, and nonfiction written by and about African Americans

CLASSROOM EXERCISES

1. Choose one of the trials mentioned in this section (that of Nat Turner, Dred Scott, or the freedom fighters of *Amistad*) and stage a reenactment. Students must become familiar with and articulate the key issues that concern the case and its historical significance for the African-American struggle.
2. Have students choose a biblical story, interpret it from the vantage point of an enslaved person, and share their interpretation with the class.
3. Have students write their own Manifesto or "Appeal" from an integrationist and/or a black nationalist perspective. Students should share their writings with the class as though they are giving a public speech.

MEDIA AND INTERNET RESOURCES

Films

Africans in America series (PBS, 1998), *Amistad* (Spielberg, 1997), *Breaking The Ice: The Mary Ann Shadd Story* (Sweeney, 2001), *Burn!* (Pontecorvo, 1969), *The Civil War* series (PBS, Ken Burns, 1989), *Glory* (Zwick, 1989), *Half Slave, Half Free* (1991), *Mandingo* (Fleischer, 1975), *The Massachusetts 59th Colored Infantry* (PBS, 1991), *The Middle Passage* (HBO, 2002), *Nat Turner: A Troublesome Property* (Burnett, 2003), *Night John* (Burnett, 1996), *Roots* (Chomsky & Erman, 1977), *Roots of Resistance* (PBS, 1989), *Sankofa* (Gerima, 1993), *Slavery & the Making of America* (James, 2004), *A Son of Africa: The Slave Narrative of Olaudah Equiano* (Aimimage Productions, 1995), *Traces of the Trade: A Story from the Deep North* (Browne, 2008), *A Woman Called Moses* (Wendkos, 1978)

Websites

"Abolitionism, 1830–1850"
http://www.iath.virginia.edu/utc/abolitn/abhp.html

"Africans in America"
http://www.pbs.org/wgbh/aia/home.html
"American Slave Narratives: An Online Anthology"
http://xroads.virginia.edu/%7Ehyper/wpa/wpahome.html
"The Atlantic Slave Trade and Slave Life in the Americas: A Visual Record"
http://hitchcock.itc.virginia.edu/Slavery/index.php
"The Church in the Southern Black Community"
http://docsouth.unc.edu/church/
"The Underground Railroad"
http://www.nationalgeographic.com/railroad/j1.html
"The Unrighteous Traffick: A Special Report by the *Providence Journal*"
http://www.projo.com/extra/2006/slavery/

SECTION TWO

RECONSTRUCTION AND REACTION

The Aftermath of Slavery and the Dawn of Segregation, 1861–1915

KEY POINTS

- Referring to the period immediately following the Civil War, the Reconstruction era was a period in which African Americans and their white allies struggled to extend full democratic rights to black people in the United States. This included fighting not only for democratic participation in government through universal male suffrage and holding political office, but also for the basic educational skills and economic resources needed to transform the conditions of the formerly enslaved.
- In this concerted effort to take advantage of the opening that the Northern victory and abolition offered, African Americans fought against reactionaries who succeeded in eroding their political and civil rights. With the Compromise of 1877, in which federal troops were withdrawn from the South, African Americans were left to the mercy of former slave owners. Black people were eliminated from state legislatures, ejected from the U.S. Congress, trapped in the sharecropping system (which often degenerated into debt peonage), excluded from public accommodations, residentially segregated, denied access to education and other essential services, denied the protection of the justice system, and terrorized by racist white mobs.

- Two major responses to the institutionalization of Jim Crow segregation were the strategies of political accommodation and self-help represented by Booker T. Washington's Tuskegee Machine and liberal integrationist militancy reflected in the National Association for the Advancement of Colored People (NAACP), led by W. E. B. Du Bois.
- Carrying on the legacy of resistance to racial and gender oppression, women of African descent established local associations that promoted racial uplift and addressed women's rights. Black women were in the forefront of the anti-lynching campaign, the effort to end the convict-leasing system, and the repeal of Jim Crow car laws.
- Due to the severe economic exploitation that they suffered, African-American workers organized the Colored National Labor Union and efforts were made to encourage black people to join workers' movements. However, racism was a significant barrier to constructing multiracial trade unions and the development of a movement that bridged the political divide between a race-conscious movement and the class struggle of workers' movements.

COMPREHENSION AND THOUGHT QUESTIONS

1. "What the Black Man Wants," *Frederick Douglass, 1865*
   a. Who is Douglass's audience in this document?
   b. How does Douglass define freedom and why?
   c. What does Douglass advocate as needed in order to actualize true freedom?
   d. What reasons does Douglass give for extending suffrage to black men?
   e. Explain the relationship that Douglass describes between the notion of racial inferiority and oppression.
2. Henry McNeal Turner, Black Christian Nationalist
   a. Within what institutions did Turner rise to leadership and prominence?
   b. Who appointed Turner the first black U.S. Army Chaplain?
   c. To whom and under what circumstances does Turner make this address?
   d. What is Turner protesting?

3. Black Urban Workers during Reconstruction
    a. Why did large numbers of African Americans migrate to the North after the Civil War?
    b. Why were labor conditions in the North difficult?
    c. What city contained the largest proportion of skilled African-American labor in the United States in 1870? How did this come about?
    d. What was the role of the trade union in the experience of African-American workers?
    e. How did the skilled laborers respond to labor conditions in Maryland?
4. "Labor and Capital Are in Deadly Conflict," *T. Thomas Fortune, 1886*
    a. What nineteenth-century philosopher and political economist was a great influence on T. Thomas Fortune?
    b. What evidence does Fortune present to support the claim that labor and capital are in deadly conflict?
    c Does Fortune suggest a resolution to this conflict? If so, what does he suggest?
5. Edward Wilmot Blyden and the African Diaspora
    a. Describe the theory of Pan-Africanism. How is this theory in evidence in Edward Wilmot Blyden's personal history?
    b. What text does Blyden use to interpret world events and conditions?
    c. What problems did abolitionists and colonists address?
    d. What are the three phases of the "Negro problem" according to Blyden?
    e. What similarities and differences exist between European and African-American colonists?
6. "The Democratic Idea Is Humanity," *Alexander Crummell, 1888*
    a. In which three countries did Alexander Crummell live?
    b. For whom was he a mentor?
    c. What organization did he establish in 1897?
    d. What is Crummell's understanding of race and how does this understanding support his argument for the civil and political equality of all peoples?
7. "A Voice from the South," *Anna Julia Cooper, 1892*
    a. In what institutions was Anna Julia Cooper educated?

b. What is the significance of her 1892 book *A Voice from the South*?
c. According to Cooper, what is the role that women must play in American society?
d. What racial differences does she observe in the area of gender relations?

8. The National Association of Colored Women: Mary Church Terrell and Josephine St. Pierre Ruffin
   a. What attributes does Mary Church Terrell ascribe to women of African descent and against what accusations is she defending them?
   b. What profession did women dominate? What significance does this have to the progress of the race?
   c. In what social issues were women of African descent involved?
   d. How does Josephine St. Pierre Ruffin characterize the relationship between northern and southern white women in the post–Civil War South?
   e. How does Ruffin represent the formerly enslaved population and how does this compare with Terrell's representation?
9. "I Know Why the Caged Bird Sings," *Paul Laurence Dunbar*
   a. Why do you think that Dunbar was best known for his "dialect poetry"?
   b. Choose one of the three poems in this section and explain how its message is relevant to the circumstances that people of African descent confronted during the era under consideration in this section.
10. Booker T. Washington and the Politics of Accommodation
   a. What institution did Booker T. Washington found and why was it significant?
   b. What did Washington promote to be the solution to the "Negro problem"?
   c. How would you characterize Washington's representation of people of African descent in his Atlanta Exposition address? What are the advantages and disadvantages of this characterization?
   d. What were Washington's arguments against legal segregation?
11. William Monroe Trotter and the *Boston Guardian*
   a. Why was William Monroe Trotter such a vehement critic of Booker T. Washington?

   b. Why were the black press and the black leaders silent in response to Washington's statements praising southern constitutions?
12. Race and the Southern Worker
   a. What are the ironies and hypocrisies of southern daily life identified by the author of "A Negro Woman Speaks"?
   b. How does the author of "The Race Question a Class Question" support the argument that racial inequality is rooted in class conflict?
   c. What are the white southern workers' objections to socialism and how does the author of "The Race Question a Class Question" resolve these concerns?
   d. What condition unites white and black workers?
13. Ida B. Wells-Barnett, Crusader for Justice
   a. What profession did Ida B. Wells-Barnett practice?
   b. What was the true motivation for the rise of the lynch-law movement in the South?
   c. What solution does Wells-Barnett propose to stop lynching and why?
14. William Edward Burghardt Du Bois
   a. What field did W. E. B. Du Bois's research establish?
   b. With which organizations and movement was he most closely associated?
   c. How does Du Bois propose that the African-American dilemma over racial and national identity be resolved?
   d. Explain the significance of "double-consciousness."
15. The Niagara Movement, *1905*
   a. Why did some intellectuals and leaders join the Niagara Movement?
   b. Identify three of the guiding principles of this movement. Briefly explain how these principles are evident in the declaration of their demands and duties.
16. Hubert Henry Harrison, Black Revolutionary Nationalist
   a. What was Hubert Henry Harrison's political philosophy?
   b. What led Harrison to become a black nationalist?
   c. What are the differences between chattel slavery and what Harrison terms "wage slavery"?

d. If class prejudice is the basis for race prejudice, why does upward economic mobility fail to alleviate racism?
e. How does Harrison understand the relationship between class and race?

ESSAY QUESTIONS

1. How are religious themes used in the African-American struggle for human rights in the United States? Draw examples from six of the excerpts in this section.
2. Review and comment on the arguments for the colonization project. What problems would colonization solve and what problems would it create?
3. Drawing on examples in the text as well as your own historical knowledge, discuss the relationship between black participation in U.S. military actions and access to full citizenship for African Americans. What have been the arguments around this issue?
4. Compare and contrast the ideologies of integration and accommodation. How does each promote or prevent the realization of democracy and freedom in the United States?
5. Imagine that you are a newly emancipated person in the United States. What conditions would you face and which would be your greatest concerns? Explain why you would or would not become involved in black nationalism, the labor movement, the Tuskegee Institute, and the Niagara Movement.
6. Identify the organizations and movements in which African-American women were most active. Why do you think that they gravitated toward these activities? How did their activism address their concerns and beliefs about the specific situation of black women?

SUGGESTED RESEARCH TOPICS

1. The political history of the Reconstruction Era
2. The formation and development of white terrorist organizations and the history of lynch law in the United States

3. The historical relationship between racial oppression and the incarceration system
4. "Double-consciousness" and African-American identity
5. The education of African Americans in the post–Civil War era
6. Institution of Jim Crow Laws in the South
7. African Americans and the Labor Movement

CLASSROOM EXERCISES

1. Facilitate a discussion examining students' understandings of the various definitions of democracy given by a number of people in the text. Then, have students write their own definition of democracy (no more than a paragraph) and break up into pairs to discuss what they have written. Questions that they may ask each other might include how they came to have such a definition, how their understanding of democracy is evident in daily life, what aspects of society contradict their definition, and the relationship between democracy and economic conditions. Each student can then briefly present what she learned from the discussion.
2. Divide the class into two groups and stage a debate between those who argue that the race question is really a class question and those who argue that race is the most critical factor facing people of African descent in the United States.
3. Have students imagine that they are journalists and key figures during this time. The journalists should create questions based on this historical context and then interview the students who are the key figures. The students playing the key figures should answer the questions based on how they think the key figures would answer. These interviews can be staged in class.
4. Create a newspaper based on the political views discussed in this section. Divide the class into small groups based on various political viewpoints; each group should determine the sections of the paper and create the content for the sections. Students can include cartoons, interviews from Classroom Exercise 3, poetry, news stories that cover major events during the time, and so on.

MEDIA AND INTERNET RESOURCES

Films

The Autobiography of Miss Jane Pitman (Korty, 1973), *The Black Press: Soldier's without Words* (CA Newsreel, 1998), *Ethnic Notions* (CA Newsreel, 1989), *Ida B. Wells: A Passion for Justice* (Greaves, 1998), *I'll Make Me a World* (PBS, 1998), *In the White Man's Image* (PBS, 1989), *One Woman, One Vote*, Vols. 1 & 2 (PBS, 1995), *The Niagara Movement: Black Protest Reborn: Resource Kit* (ASALH, 2005, CD-ROM), *When Democracy Works* (Aubin Pictures)

Websites

"Black American Feminism: A Multidisciplinary Bibliography"
http://www.library.ucsb.edu/blackfeminism
"A Curriculum of United States Labor History for Teachers"
http://www.kentlaw.edu/ilhs/curricul.htm
"An Outline of the Reconstruction Era"
http://chnm.gmu.edu/courses//122/recon/reconframe.html
"Picture History: Reconstruction Era"
http://www.picturehistory.com/category/cat_id/6/subcat_id/176/page/6
"Without Sanctuary: Photographs and Postcards of Lynching in America"
http://www.withoutsanctuary.org/
"Women and Social Movements in the United States: 1775–2000"
http://womhist.alexanderstreet.com/

SECTION THREE

FROM PLANTATION TO GHETTO

The Great Migration, Harlem Renaissance, and World War, 1915–1954

KEY POINTS

- Jim Crow segregation was the general political reality for African Americans during this period in which the governmental authorities of the United States denied full citizenship to racialized minorities. This state-sponsored racism was accompanied by and necessarily complicit with the terrorism inflicted upon African Americans by white racist mobs both in and outside of the South.
- The Great Migration entailed the movement of millions of African Americans from the South to the Northeast, Midwest, and Far West. This migration was motivated by economic factors such as the mechanization of agriculture, the decline of cotton farming, the presence of better-paying industrial jobs in the North, and the racial and political persecution of the South. Many thriving black urban centers were created as a result of this mass movement of the population.
- A political shift occurred in which the competing dominant political ideologies within the national black community were no longer accommodationism versus integrationism, but integrationism and black nationalism. W. E. B. Du Bois continued to lead the liberal integrationist movement and Marcus Garvey emerged as the principal spokesperson for black nationalism. After Booker T. Washington's death, the NAACP

soon became the leading voice of the black middle class, reflecting a philosophy of liberal integrationism. The liberal integrationists were challenged, however, by black nationalism, represented by Marcus Garvey and the newly emerging radicalism of black socialists such as A. Philip Randolph and black activists in the Communist Party.

- With Garvey's imprisonment and the decline of the Universal Negro Improvement Association (UNIA) in the late 1920s, and the inadequacy of the NAACP in addressing the crisis precipitated by the Great Depression, a third political route that combined race militancy and class struggle emerged. Radical workers, intellectuals, leaders, organizers, and organizations promoted transformationism and advocated for the dismantling of institutional racism, the democratization of the U.S. state, the fundamental redistribution of wealth, and the elimination of all social manifestations of race and gender inequality.
- World War II, which gave way to the Cold War, dealt a debilitating blow to the American Left as millions of radical workers, intellectuals, and artists were expelled from unions, dismissed from educational institutions, imprisoned, and forbidden to travel.

COMPREHENSION AND THOUGHT QUESTIONS

1. Black Conflict over World War I
   a. What were the two conflicting interpretations of World War I?
   b. Why does Harrison criticize Du Bois's articulation of the position that African Americans should take regarding the war?
   c. Why do you think Du Bois encouraged African Americans to support the war?
2. "If We Must Die," *Claude McKay, 1919*
   a. What inspired much of Claude McKay's poetry and essays?
   b. How would you describe the mood of "If We Must Die"?
   c. How does this poem address the conditions faced by African Americans in the beginning of the twentieth century?
   d. Do you find this poem to be powerful? Why or why not?
3. Black Bolsheviks: Cyril V. Briggs and Claude McKay
   a. What organization did Briggs organize and what was its primary goal?

   b. Why do you think members of this organization were critical of the NAACP and the concept of the "talented tenth"?
   c. According to Briggs, what are the manifestations and consequences of racism in the labor movement?
   d. What is the relationship between the Great Migration and the rise of the black Left?
   e. Why does McKay advocate for the dissemination of propaganda on African-American grievances?
   f. Why do you think McKay went to Russia? Explain why he compares the position of African Americans and that of the lower classes and minorities of the Old Russia.
4. Marcus Garvey and the Universal Negro Improvement Association
   a. What African-American leader inspired Marcus Garvey and why?
   b. As an international movement, in what areas of the world was the UNIA was based? Why do you think it was an international movement?
   c. What problems did the Garvey movement seek to address?
   d. According to Garvey, what is race prejudice?
   e. What sources of division within the black race does Garvey identify?
5. "Women as Leaders," *Amy Euphemia Jacques Garvey, 1925*
   a. What was Amy Garvey's role in the Garvey movement?
   b. What is Garvey's vision of women's place in society?
   c. To what does she attribute the differing levels of achievement of black and white women?
6. Langston Hughes and the Harlem Renaissance
   a. What project were writers, artists, and musicians in Harlem attempting to undertake?
   b. What themes does Langston Hughes explore in his work?
   c. According to Hughes, why would it be difficult for a middle-class black artist to be interested in black subjects?
   d. What is essential for a truly great artist?
   e. Do you agree with Hughes's characterization of the "common element"? Why or why not?
   f. Summarize Hughes's explanation of the predicament of the Negro artist.

c. What evidence does Hughes provide to support his claim that the economic color line is more predominant and severe than the social or political one?

7. "The Negro Woman and the Ballot," *Alice Moore Dunbar-Nelson, 1927*
   a. In which professions did Alice Dunbar-Nelson work?
   b. What do the arguments used by women in their struggle for the right to vote reveal about gender relations?
   c. On what issues was the vote of African-American women particularly influential?
   d. How can African-American women better use their vote according to Dunbar-Nelson?
8. James Weldon Johnson and Harlem in the 1920s
   a. What were two of James Weldon Johnson's greatest accomplishments?
   b. What motivated African Americans to move to different parts of the city?
   c. What were the mechanisms of residential segregation in New York described by Johnson?
   d. What does Johnson predict regarding the fate of Harlem? Why does he believe that African Americans are less economically threatened in Harlem?
9. Black Workers in the Great Depression
   a. What was the unemployment rate for African Americans in the labor force during the Great Depression? How do you think that this affected daily life in a community such as Harlem?
   b. What was the cause of bitterness between black and white workers?
   c. What does Harris suggest must happen in order to overcome obstacles to the unification of black and white labor?
10. The Scottsboro Trials, *1930s*
    a. Of what crime were the "Scottsboro Boys" accused?
    b. What is the significance of the Scottsboro trial?
    c. Toward what audience or audiences do you think the Scottsboro Boys' appeal is directed? Why?

11. "You Cannot Kill the Working Class," *Angelo Herndon, 1933*
    a. What was Angelo Herndon's political ideology? Why was he arrested?
    b. What was so momentous about the 1932 demonstration at the Atlanta courthouse building?
    c. Explain why Herndon claims that there would still be a race question if there were no African Americans in the United States. Do you agree with him? Why or why not?
    d. How do you think Herndon's personal experiences shaped his political ideology and work?
12. Hosea Hudson, Black Communist Activist
    a. Why did the Communist Party appeal to Hosea Hudson?
    b. What means did companies and the state use to control workers?
13. "Breaking the Bars to Brotherhood," *Mary McCleod Bethune, 1935*
    a. With what organizations is Mary McCleod Bethune associated?
    b. What does Bethune fear will happen to the black man in America and why?
    c. Why do you think Bethune states that "the creed of freedom has not yet been written"?
14. Adam Clayton Powell, Jr., and the Fight for Black Employment in Harlem
    a. What campaign did Adam Clayton Powell, Jr., lead during the Depression?
    b. What did this campaign use as leverage to force businesses to end discriminatory hiring policies?
15. Black Women Workers during the Great Depression
    a. How did the exploitation of labor in the cotton industry affect women?
    b. Why did landlords let farms to sharecroppers with the largest families?
    c. How would you describe the relationship between the sharecroppers' families and the landowners' families?
    d. How do the experiences of Naomi Ward speak to the experience of oppression on the basis of class, race, and gender?

16. Southern Negro Youth Conference, *1939*
    a. What were the goals of the participants in the Southern Negro Youth Conference?
    b. Why was the growth of organized labor in the South considered a source of hope?
17. A. Philip Randolph and the Negro March on Washington Movement, *1941*
    a. What organization did A. Philip Randolph help to found?
    b. Why was the Negro March on Washington movement being planned in 1941?
    c. What was one of the dilemmas of the black worker and how did Randolph propose that this dilemma could be solved?
    d. What dilemma faced by people of African descent was highlighted during World War II?
    e. What parallel does Randolph draw between the United States and Germany?
18. Charles Hamilton Houston and the War Effort among African Americans, *1944*
    a. What was Charles Hamilton Houston's contribution to the modern Civil Rights movement?
    b. Why does the treatment of African Americans in the armed forces serve as a particularly powerful example in the struggle for desegregation?
    c. What does Houston claim to be the effect of U.S. racial segregation in the international community?
19. "An End to the Neglect of the Problems of the Negro Woman!" *Claudia Jones, 1949*
    a. Claudia Jones was involved in activities regarding what issues?
    b. Why was Jones expelled from the United States?
    c. According to Jones, why has there been an intensification of oppression of African-American women?
    d. To what does Jones attribute the gulf that exists between African American and white death rates?
    e. How does Jones account for the subordination of African-American women?

f. Do Jones's examples of white chauvinism sufficiently explain African-American women's insufficient participation in progressive organizations? Why or why not?
g. How do Jones's ideas about the connections between gender, race, and class compare with analyses of gender by Anna Julia Cooper and Amy Jacques Garvey?

20. "The Negro Artist Looks Ahead," *Paul Robeson, 1951*
    a. Why was Paul Robeson forbidden to travel in 1950?
    b. How did Robeson combine his artistic talent with his social activism?
    c. Why was it important to Robeson that non-elite people have access to art?
    d. How did Robeson understand the role and responsibilities of the artist in public life?
21. Thurgood Marshall: The *Brown* Decision and the Struggle for School Desegregation
    a. What is the importance of the *Brown* decision?
    b. Why was Marshall's appointment to and presence on the U.S. Supreme Court significant?
    c. What theory underlies racial segregation?
    d. What examples of progress in the struggle to "remove race and cast from American life" does Marshall provide? How do you think that citing such examples helped to support Marshall's argument for full desegregation?

ESSAY QUESTIONS

1. How do artists and activists featured in this section address issues of class within the African-American community? What are their commentaries, critiques, and recommendations?
2. Describe daily life under Jim Crow segregation from the perspective of both a black and white person. In what ways did Jim Crow affect the lives of members in each group?
3. According to the material in this section, what was the impact of World War I on race relations in the United States?

4. Explain the relationship between racial injustice and economic exploitation as the authors in this section articulate it. How did the activism of groups and individuals seek to bring about racial equality and rights for working-class people?
5. What was the role of political organizing in addressing the problems of this era?
6. What conditions did World War II create or exacerbate that contributed to the emergence of the modern Civil Rights movement?
7. The persecution of African-American activists figures prominently in the struggle for equality and justice. Identify instances of such persecution and explore their causes and consequences. What are the implications for U.S. democracy?

SUGGESTED RESEARCH TOPICS

1. The international labor movements of the early twentieth century
2. The impact of international migration on African-American communities
3. Artists of the Harlem Renaissance
4. The rise and fall of the Universal Negro Improvement Association
5. The history of African-American participation in World War I and World War II
6. The role of people from the Caribbean in the African-American struggle
7. African Americans and the Communist Party

CLASSROOM EXERCISES

1. Have students locate and read interviews of people who lived through the Great Depression (or interview someone who themselves or whose parents lived during the Great Depression) and present their findings from this material to the class for discussion. Compare the experiences of interviewees based on their race, ethnicity, gender, and class backgrounds.
2. Have students choose a writer or musician from the Harlem Renaissance and introduce this person to the class through both biographical

information and a presentation of his or her work. For example, students may choose to recite poems by Langston Hughes, read an excerpt from one of Zora Neale Hurston's short stories, sing the *Negro National Anthem* by James Weldon Johnson, play a jazz document by a Renaissance musician, and so on.

MEDIA AND INTERNET RESOURCES

Films

Against the Odds: Artists of the Harlem Renaissance (PBS), *American Visions: Streamlines and Breadlines* (PBS, 1997), *Goin' to Chicago* (on the Great Migration, CA Newsreel, 1994), An Interview with Hosea Hudson (Wilson & Schomburg Center for Research on Black Culture, 1983), *A Lynching in Marion* (PBS, 1995), *Marcus Garvey: Look for Me in the Whirlwind* (PBS, Nelson, 2000), *Miles of Smiles/Years of Troubles* (on the Pullman Porters' Union, CA Newsreel, 1983), *Mood Indigo: Blacks and Whites—America Goes to War: The Home Front* (PBS, 1989), *Oh Free-dom after While: The Missouri Sharecroppers' Strike of 1939* (CA Newsreel, Ross, 1999), *Paul Robeson: Portraits of the Artist* (Murphy & MacPherson 2007), *The Road to Brown* (Elwood & Kulish, 1990), *Scottsboro: An American Tragedy* (Akner & Goodman, 2000), *Second American Revolution*, Parts 1 & 2 (PBS, 1984), *Trouble Behind* (CA Newsreel, 1990), *The Tuskegee Airmen: They Fought Two Wars* (PBS, 2003), *Zora Neale Hurston: Jump at the Sun* (Pollard, 2008)

Websites

"African American Mosaic: A Library of Congress Resource Guide for the Study of Black History and Culture"
http://www.loc.gov/exhibits/african/afam008.html
"African American Odyssey: A Quest for Full Citizenship"
http://memory.loc.gov/ammem/aaohtml/exhibit/aoover.html
"Harlem 1900–1940: An African American Community"
http://www.si.umich.edu/CHICO/Harlem/

"The History of Jim Crow"
http://jimcrowhistory.org/home.htm
"The Jacob Lawrence Virtual Archive and Education Center"
http://www.jacoblawrence.org
"Selected Women Writers of the Harlem Renaissance: A Resource Guide"
http://www.nku.edu/~diesmanj/guides/index.html
"Virtual Jim Crow Museum"
http://www.ferris.edu/news/jimcrow/index.htm

SECTION FOUR

WE SHALL OVERCOME

The Second Reconstruction, 1954–1975

KEY POINTS

- The 1954 *Brown v. Board of Education* decision that determined racial segregation in public schools to be unlawful represented a legal victory in the broader campaign to dismantle racial segregation and thereby restructure social and political life in the United States.
- The successful desegregation of U.S. society represented by dramatic political victories must be considered in the larger context of the socioeconomic, cultural, and political metamorphosis of U.S. race relations. The significance of the black presence in all aspects of American life—from sports and art to politics and the economy—received recognition and the destruction of legal segregation became inevitable.
- The victories of the Black Freedom movement must also be considered in the context of the major shift in global politics that followed World War II. The United States and the Soviet Union emerged as the two competing superpowers, and legal racial segregation discredited the United States' claim to be the bearer of democracy. As countries in Africa, Asia, and the Caribbean became newly decolonized nations, the United States sought to make them political and economic allies in the fight against communism and for global domination. The policy of legal white supremacy was no longer tenable given these changing geopolitical issues.

- The Black Freedom movement was a broad-based united front, which consisted roughly of those who wanted to assimilate within the system, those who were committed to social protest against the system, and those who sought to fundamentally transform the social and economic system associated with racial and gender oppression.
- Legislative victories did not lead to fundamental transformation and thus the Black Power movement replaced liberal integrationism as the dominant popular political ideology and discourse for African Americans for nearly a decade, but never consolidated itself as a coherent social philosophy or strategy.

COMPREHENSION AND THOUGHT QUESTIONS

1. Rosa Parks, Jo Ann Robinson, and the Montgomery Bus Boycott, *1955–1956*
   a. What was Jo Ann Robinson's role in the Montgomery Bus Boycott?
   b. What was the Women's Political Council? Why is it significant?
   c. What impact do you think that the existence of a reserved section for whites only had on white bus passengers? Why?
   d. What factors do you think allowed the Boycott to be successful?
   e. What influence did the *Brown* ruling have on the Montgomery Bus Boycott?
2. Roy Wilkins and the NAACP
   a. What accounted for the declining influence of Roy Wilkins and the NAACP?
   b. To what does Wilkins attribute the increasing racial tension that followed the *Brown* decision?
   c. What were White Citizens' Councils? Why do you think that whites went to extreme measures to preserve segregation, given that blacks held relatively little power in the South?
   d. Why does Wilkins compare police action in Montgomery with Soviet Communism? Do you think that this comparison is valid?
3. The Southern Christian Leadership Conference (SCLC), *1957*
   a. How was the SCLC different from the NAACP?
   b. What are the goals of the SCLC?

   c. How did Gandhi influence the SCLC?
   d. What were the obstacles that prevented African Americans in the South from voting and how did SCLC combat these obstacles?
   e. How does the SCLC define an "unjust law"? How would you define an "unjust law"?
   f. What impact does segregation have on black and white people?
4. Student Nonviolent Coordinating Committee (SNCC) and the Sit-In-Movement, *1960*
   a. What was the SNCC's primary focus?
   b. Who were the leaders associated with the SNCC?
   c. What factors contributed to the SNCC becoming more radical?
   d. Why was non-violence a powerful tool to end segregation?
   e. Do you think that this is an effective strategy in achieving fundamental social change? Why or why not?
5. Freedom Songs, *1960s*
   a. What functions did freedom songs serve?
   b. What were the sources of freedom songs?
   c. In reading the lyrics of the two songs in this section, what do you think are the obstacles to freedom and how do people intend to combat them?
   d. Compare the ideas expressed in the freedom songs with the music and artistic expressions reflected in the Harlem Renaissance during the 1920s.
6. "We Need Group-Centered Leadership," *Ella Baker*
   a. In what positions did Ella Baker develop and utilize her skills as a community organizer and activist?
   b. What are the similarities between the reasons that she left the NAACP and the SCLC?
   c. How did the insistence on group-centered leadership echo the overall objectives of the Civil Rights movement?
7. Martin Luther King, Jr., and Nonviolence
   a. What international prize was Martin Luther King, Jr., awarded in 1964?
   b. What were King's ethical and economic philosophies?
   c. What was King planning to launch at the time of his 1968 assassination?

d. What examples exist that contradict King's characterization of the African American as patiently accepting injustice and exploitation prior to the 1950s?
e. Why do you think that King linked the black movement in the United States with the international freedom struggle?
f. Do you think that King's dream has been realized? Why or why not?

8. "The Revolution Is at Hand," *John R. Lewis, 1963*
   a. Why was Lewis's speech censored?
   b. What is the significance of the changes that were made (see endnotes in the anthology)?
   c. In what ways does Lewis make a connection between economic justice and civil rights?
9. "The Salvation of American Negroes Lies in Socialism," *W. E. B. Du Bois*
   a. Why was W. E. B. Du Bois dismissed from the NAACP in the 1940s?
   b. How did Du Bois's political ideology change?
   c. What is the central idea of socialism?
   d. According to Du Bois, what is the relationship between the development of industry and the ruin of democracy?
   e. What is the program of the United States to which Du Bois refers on page 390? How has the majority of America been convinced to go along with this program?
   f. What is Du Bois's critique of American culture? Do you agree with it? Why or why not?
10. "The Special Plight and the Role of Black Women," *Fannie Lou Hamer*
   a. How do you think Fannie Lou Hamer's personal background influenced her political activism?
   b. Why does Hamer say that she was "tickled" when people talked about integration?
   c. How does Hamer relate the struggle of black women to that of white women?
   d. Explain the significance of "Up-South" and "Down-South."

11. "SNCC Position Paper: Women in the Movement," *1964*
    a. What are examples of women being denied leadership positions and authority in the Civil Rights movement?
    b. What parallel do the authors of this paper make between racial and gender subjugation? Do you think it is effective? Why or why not?
    c. What contradiction in the movement does this paper implicate?
12. Elijah Muhammad and the Nation of Islam
    a. How did Elijah Muhammad come to lead the Nation of Islam?
    b. What demands do members of the Nation of Islam make that are similar to other groups involved in the freedom movement? What is different?
    c. Why are members of the Nation of Islam against integration?
13. Malcolm X and Revolutionary Black Nationalism
    a. Why did Malcolm X leave the Nation of Islam?
    b. In what way was Malcolm X's political and ideological perspective changing at the time of his assassination?
    c. According to Malcolm X, what unites black people regardless of political ideology, religion, or class background?
    d. Why doesn't Malcolm X consider himself to be an American? Do you agree with his argument? Why or why not?
    e. Why is Malcolm X critical of the Democratic Party in particular and the U.S. government in general?
    f. Why does Malcolm X agree to work on school desegregation despite his position on integration?
    g. How would you summarize the goals of the Organization for Afro-American Unity?
14. Black Power
    a. What brought about the emergence of the Black Power movement?
    b. What is the significance of the Black Power slogan? Why did "Power" become a necessary part of Black Freedom movement discourse?
    c. What are ways in which the vote can be used for social change?
    d. How is Ella Baker's philosophy of group-centered leadership evidenced in Stokely Carmichael's document?

e. According to Carmichael, why is there a need for all-black organizations in the freedom movement? Why must blacks cut themselves off from whites in order to proceed toward true liberation?
f. What is Bayard Rustin's critique of Black Power? What contradictions does he point out?
g. What solution does Rustin offer to the problem of enacting true social change?

15. "CORE Endorses Black Power," *Floyd McKissick, 1967*
    a. What was "Soul City"? How did Floyd McKissick secure funding for this project?
    b. McKissick states that the belief in black inferiority that allowed human slavery to occur has been quietly reinforced. Do you agree with this? Why or why not?
    c. What is to blame for the rebellions, according to McKissick? Why?
    d. Why does McKissick resent so-called Negro leaders?
16. "To Atone for Our Sins and Errors in Vietnam," *Martin Luther King, Jr., 1967*
    a. In what ways were Martin Luther King's politics in the years just prior to his assassination more radical?
    b. What connection does King make between the war in Vietnam and the struggle that he and others have been waging in the United States? Why does he say that the war is a cruel manipulation of the poor?
    c. What reasons does King provide to explain the distrust the Vietnamese have for the United States? Why does he provide this perspective?
    d. Some historians divide King's career into two phases: the early King who led desegregation campaigns and the later King who fought against war, poverty, and racism. When Americans today celebrate Dr. King's birthday, which King do they celebrate, and why?
17. Huey P. Newton and the Black Panther Party for Self-Defense
    a. How did the Black Panther Party gain support within black urban communities? Why did they patrol the streets of Oakland?

b. What were the factors that lead to the decline of the Black Panther Party?
c. What is the significance of forty acres and two mules?
d. What problems do the rules of the Black Panther Party attempt to address?
e. What is Huey P. Newton's vision of the Black Panther Party? What are its most fundamental principles? Support your answer with examples from the text.

18. "The People Have to Have the Power," *Fred Hampton*
a. What is the significance of the year 1967 to the Black Freedom movement?
b. Why does Hampton relate racial and economic oppression?
c. Many researchers state that the Chicago police were responsible for Hampton's murder. How did Hampton's ideas challenge governmental and police authorities?

19. "I Am a Revolutionary Black Woman," *Angela Y. Davis, 1970*
a. How did Angela Y. Davis come to be an international figure in the Black Freedom movement?
b. To which political and social ideologies has Davis contributed?
c. What reasons does Davis provide for being a Communist?
d. According to Davis, what is the relationship between black liberation and women's liberation?
e. What does Davis believe to be the true reason that she was put on trial?
f. How do Davis's ideas parallel those expressed by Claudia Jones?

20. "Our Thing Is DRUM!" *The League of Revolutionary Black Workers*
a. What is the legacy of the League of Revolutionary Black Workers?
b. How did the League understand the failures of the white labor movement? What reasons does the League give for its inadequacies?
c. What are the crimes of U.S. imperialism according to the League? Do you believe these accusations have any validity? Why or why not?
d. Comment on the League's short- and long-term objectives.

21. Attica: "The Fury of Those Who Are Oppressed," *1971*
a. Why did the prisoners of Attica revolt?

b. Why do you think that the inmates requested to be under federal jurisdiction?
c. Do you think that the inmates' demands and proposals should have been considered? Why or why not?

22. The National Black Political Convention, Gary, Indiana, *March 1972*
    a. What were the objectives of the participants in the Gary Convention?
    b. What are the crisis conditions to which the convention was responding?
    c. What were the choices that Gary participants had with regards to social action? Why were these said to be the only "real choices"?
    d. What do the authors of the document mean when they state that they "stand on the edge of history"? What is at stake and why?
23. "There Is No Revolution without the People," *Amiri Baraka, 1972*
    a. In what ways has Amiri Baraka combined his artistic talent with his political activism?
    b. How does Baraka interpret the notion of "Back-to-Africa"?
    c. What is the Congress of African People? How does Baraka propose it go about achieving its goals?
    d. Why does Baraka emphasize the need for Pan-Africanist and black nationalist involvement in local politics?
    e. Compare and contrast Baraka's views of the role of the artist with those of Paul Robeson's.
24. "My Sight Is Gone but My Vision Remains," *Henry Winston*
    a. What is ironic about Winston's personal history?
    b. What is the significance of the title of this section?
    c. What did Winston believe were some of the actions and interests of U.S. imperialism? Why is this relevant to the Black Freedom movement in the United States?

ESSAY QUESTIONS

1. The material from this as well as previous sections indicates that the relationship between individual states and the federal government has been critical to the African-American struggle for rights. Identify ex-

amples and discuss the ways in which the balance (or imbalance) of power between state and federal governments has impacted the daily lives of African Americans.

2. What were some of the contradictions within the Black Freedom movement? How do you think that they might have affected the success of the movement?
3. Both Martin Luther King, Jr., and Malcolm X were assassinated at a time when they began to develop a more international perspective on the condition of African Americans. What are the implications of each leader's changing perspective?
4. What do authors in this section suggest about the possibilities of bridging class, gender, and color differences to achieve the goal of a just society?
5. What is the political, economic, and social philosophy of black nationalism? How does it contradict integrationism? Use excerpts from this section to argue for or against black nationalism as a solution to the problems that face people of African descent in the United States. How does what the editors refer to as "transformation" differ from both of these?
6. Drawing upon the material in this section, explain how the Cold War and the anti-Communist movement in the United States affected the Black Freedom movement.
7. What has been the role of the U.S. government in the repression of the Black Freedom movement?

SUGGESTED RESEARCH TOPICS

1. Women of the modern Civil Rights movement and the Black Power movement
2. The relationship between international liberation movements and the Black Freedom movement in the United States
3. The rise and fall of McCarthyism
4. COINTELPRO (Counter Intelligence Program) and the destruction of the Black Power movement
5. The Black Power movement and the arts

6. The anti-war movement
7. Activist organizations for LGBTQ (lesbian, gay, bisexual, transgender, queer) people of color

CLASSROOM EXERCISES

1. Have students develop questions and interview either a Vietnam veteran, a political activist from the period under consideration, or anyone who lived through the Civil Rights, Black Power, and anti-war movements and present the information that they learned to the class. Discuss how these personal experiences relate to the issues raised in this section.
2. Divide students into small groups and have them identify contemporary social problems and discuss the advantages and disadvantages of the various strategies of social action used during the period under consideration in this section in finding solutions to these problems. Write these problems and their solutions on the board or on an overhead presentation.

MEDIA AND INTERNET RESOURCES

Films

At the River I Stand (CA Newsreel, 1993), *Black Panthers* (Varda, 1968), *Black Panther/San Francisco State: On Strike* (CA Newsreel, 1969), *Black Theatre: The Making of a Movement* (King Jr., 1978), *Born on the Fourth of July*, *A. Philip Randolph: For Jobs and Freedom* (CA Newsreel, 1996), *Boycott* (HBO, Johnson, 2001), *Brother Outsider: The Life of Bayard Rustin* (Kates & Singer, 2002), *Eyes on the Prize* Series (PBS, 1990), *Freedom on My Mind* (CA Newsreel, 1994), *Four Little Girls* (Spike Lee, 1997), *Fundi: the Story of Ella Baker* (Icarus Films, 1986), *Malcolm X* (Spike Lee, 1992), *Mississippi, America* (PBS, 1995), *The Murder of Emmett Till* (Nelson, 2002), *The Murder of Fred Hampton* (Alk, 1978), *Nationtime, Gary* (on the First National Black Political Convention, Greaves, 1972), *Prisons on Fire: George*

Jackson, Attica & Black Liberation (AK Press, 2002, sound recording), *REVOLUTION '67* (Tibaldo-Bongiorno, 2008), *Scarred Justice: The Orangeburg Massacre 1968* (Cram & Richardson 2008), *The Strange Demise of Jim Crow* (CA Newsreel, 1998), *Thurgood Marshall: Portrait of an American Hero* (PBS, 1985), *What We Want, What We Believe: The Black Panther Party Library* (Payne, 2006)

Websites

"African Activist Archive Project"
http://africanactivist.msu.edu
"The African American Journey: The Modern Civil Rights Movement"
http://www.worldbook.com/wb/Students?content_spotlight/aajourney/civilrights
"Buffalo Soldiers"
http://www.au.af.mil/au/aul/bibs/afhist/afbuf.htm
"COINTELPRO"
http://www.icdc.com/~paulwolf/cointelpro/cointel.htm
"Civil Rights Documentation Project"
http://www.usm.edu/crdp/
"Civil Rights Movement Veterans"
http://www.crmvet.org
"The Desegregation of the Armed Forces"
http://www.trumanlibrary.org/whistlestop/study_collections/desegregation/large/desegregation.htm
"The Murder of Emmett Till"
http://www.pbs.org/wgbh/amex/till/index.html

SECTION FIVE

THE FUTURE IN THE PRESENT

Contemporary African-American Thought, 1975 to the Present

KEY POINTS

- This period has witnessed a radical transformation in black political movements and social thought due to fundamental changes within the United States and global economies. These changes include deindustrialization of advanced capitalist societies, the dismantling of the welfare state, the collapse of the Soviet Union and the international Communist movement, and the rapid expansion of the prison-industrial complex.
- There has been a realignment of the ideological spectrum of black political culture in which class stratification and internal polarization have been a dominant trend, effectively reducing the historical bonds of race-based solidarity. A central division among the integrationists has been between black conservatives, who have been strongly promoted in the media, and the liberal integrationists, best exemplified by the Rainbow Coalition.
- Revolutionary nationalism became largely marginalized as resurgence occurred in conservative black nationalism, evidenced in the rise of Molefi Asante's Afrocentricity and the Nation of Islam under Louis Farrakhan.

- The black radical agenda became increasingly advanced from the vantage point of gender as black feminists produced some of the most perceptive and critical analyses of conservative integrationists and nationalists. This tradition has also been evident in the successful antiapartheid struggle, the changes in the AFL-CIO in which African Americans have played a major role, and the birth of the Black Radical Congress.
- In the twenty-first century, American politics shifted to the Right. This shift was fueled by the 2000 election of President George W. Bush and the terrorist attacks on September 11, 2001. In reaction to the terrorist attacks, the U.S. government instated numerous laws that restricted the civil and constitutional rights of Americans and launched the "war on terror." The "war on terror" incited xenophobia and intolerance focused at Americans with Middle Eastern backgrounds or who identified as Muslim.
- Hip-hop emerged as a successful model of black political resistance. Grounded in the radical and militant traditions of the 1970s, hip-hop artists and activist youth organizations have been active in fighting the persistence of racial, social, and economic inequalities. This is most evident in the struggles around the war in Iraq and Afghanistan, the HIV/AIDS pandemic, the devastation of Hurricane Katrina, and black-on-black violence.
- The 2008 election of President Obama, which included wins in several states with white majorities, challenged right-wing politics and the structure of white privilege. Obama's race-neutral politics and colorblind cooperation have spurred questions as to whether America is moving toward a post-racial state.

COMPREHENSION AND THOUGHT QUESTIONS

1. Combahee River Collective Statement, *1977*
   a. What is the significance of the Combahee River Collective?
   b. According to this statement, what creates the conditions of black women's lives?
   c. What factors contributed to the genesis of black feminism?

   d. According to the Collective, why is feminism threatening to the majority of black people? What are the differences between the responses of most black women and men to black feminism?
2. "Women in Prison: How We Are," *Assata Shakur, 1978*
   a. Why have some writers identified Assata Shakur as a political prisoner?
   b. How and why does Shakur problematize the social structure of the prison?
   c. What differences exist between female and male prisons? Why do you think this is so?
   d. What is the role of urbanization in the conditions of women in prison, according to Shakur?
   e. Why does Shakur believe that it is imperative to the struggle to build a strong black women's movement?
   f. Compare the conditions and issues confronted by black women in prison, according to Shakur, with the situation described by Attica prisoners in 1971.
3. "It's Our Turn," *Harold Washington, 1983*
   a. What is significant about Harold Washington's mayoral career?
   b. How do the problems in Chicago that Washington identifies reflect both national and international economic changes?
   c. Why do you think Washington appealed to Chicagoans and how did he win the election?
4. "I Am Your Sister," *Audre Lorde, 1984*
   a. Explain Audre Lorde's understanding of the function of oppressed groups in society.
   b. How and why is Lorde critical of the way difference is dealt with in U.S. society?
   c. Do you agree with Lorde's analysis of why the literature of women of color was not included in women's literature classes? Why or why not?
   d. Why does Lorde see the struggle as a "war against dehumanization"? What do you think that she means by this?
   e. What have been some of the consequences of misnaming the need for unity as a need for homogeneity?

f. How does Lorde explain the treatment of black lesbians? What do you think of this explanation?

5. "Shaping Feminist Theory," *bell hooks, 1984*
   a. What is bell hooks's critique of *The Feminine Mystique*?
   b. How does hooks account for many women's reluctance to join the women's movement?
   c. Why have middle-class white women been able to define the women's movement?
   d. On page 528, hooks states, "as long as [black men and white women] or any group defines liberation as gaining social equality with ruling-class white men, they have a vested interest in the continued exploitation and oppression of others." Explain this statement. Do you agree? Why or why not?
   e. How do you think class privilege among black women affects hooks's analysis?
6. The Movement against Apartheid: Jesse Jackson and Randall Robinson
   a. What acted as a catalyst for the movement against Apartheid?
   b. Do you agree with Jackson's argument that the United States has a moral responsibility to assist in alleviating starvation and other tragedies in Africa? Why or why not?
   c. How did the United States support the political stability of the apartheid regime? What were the consequences of this support?
   d. How does the South African case exemplify the roles of the U.S. government as well as organized resistance in the international Black Freedom movement?
   e. How does African American participation in the antiapartheid movement reflect a history of African-American involvement with Africa?
7. "Keep Hope Alive," *Jesse Jackson, 1988*
   a. Why do you think Jesse Jackson evokes the names and experiences of people who came before him in the Black Freedom Movement?
   b. Upon what common ground does Jackson suggest that the Rainbow Coalition stands?
   c. Explain Jackson's critique of Reaganomics.

d. How does Jackson use his personal history to support his political message?
e. Compare the issues raised in Jackson's 1988 address with the issues cited in the black agenda at the 1972 Gary Convention.

8. "Afrocentricity," *Molefi Asante, 1991*
   a. In what arena has Asante's theory of Afrocentricity been influential?
   b. What are the differences between Afrocentricity and Eurocentricity? Why does Asante suggest that African-American children in particular will benefit from an Afrocentric education?
   c. What is multicultural education and how does Asante envision it to relate to Afrocentricity?
   d. Do you agree with Asante that the United States would be a different nation today if students had received an Afrocentric education? Why or why not?
   e. How do Asante's ideas about Afrocentricity compare with the ideas of earlier black nationalists?
9. The Anita Hill–Clarence Thomas Controversy, *1991*
   a. What does the nomination and appointment of Clarence Thomas as a replacement for Thurgood Marshall reveal about the U.S. political climate and specifically about black political culture?
   b. How is sexual harassment an issue of both gender and race?
   c. Why does Jordan believe that Anita Hill's experience exemplifies the "traditional abusive loneliness of black women in this savage society"?
10. "Race Matters," *Cornel West, 1991*
   a. What does West mean when he refers to the "structural character of culture"?
   b. Why does West call attention to the emotional, psychological, and spiritual state of much of black America? What do you think this adds to discussions about the plight of African Americans?
   c. Do you agree with West's critiques of liberal structuralists and conservative behaviorists? Why or why not?
   d. How does West account for the growth in nihilism in black America? Assuming that you agree with his assessment, what factors do

you think could account for the increasing power of the nihilistic threat?

e. What does West mean by "a politics of conversion"?
f. What are his critiques of integrationist and black nationalist strategies for change?

11. "Black Anti-Semitism," *Henry Louis Gates, Jr., 1992*
    a. Why does Henry Louis Gates argue that black anti-Semitism should not be dismissed as marginal?
    b. Gates argues that an aspect of black anti-Semitism rests on the notion that "culpability is heritable." What are the implications of his critique for past and present campaigns for reparations?
    c. To what does Gates attribute the rise in black anti-Semitism?
    d. Why is Gates so strongly opposed to what he refers to as an "isolationist" agenda?
12. "Crime—Causes and Cures," *Jarvis Tyner, 1994*
    a. To what does Jarvis Tyner attribute the growth of crime?
    b. What is the role of the media in the crime issue? What is the role of the government?
    c. How does Tyner critique the way that crime is constructed in U.S. society?
    d. According to Tyner, why haven't the death penalty, stiffer sentencing, and greater rates of incarceration solved the crime problem?
13. Louis Farrakhan: The Million Man March, *1995*
    a. What is the significance of the Million Man March?
    b. Why does Louis Farrakhan insist that black men join religious organizations?
    c. Why do you think that the Nation of Islam was so successful in organizing the Million Man March?
    d. Many observers sharply criticized the Million Man March for its exclusion of women and emphasis on patriarchy. Discuss.
14. "A Voice from Death Row," *Mumia Abu-Jamal*
    a. Why is Mumia Abu-Jamal identified as a political prisoner?
    b. What is Jamal's critique of capital punishment?
15. "Let Justice Roll Down Like Waters," *African-American Prisoners in Sing Sing, 1998*

a. As of 2003, there were more than two million Americans incarcerated in prisons and jails throughout the country. What role have prisons come to play in American society?
b. What is identified as unjust about the criminal justice system?
c. How do you think that the rise in incarceration affects daily life in the larger society?
d. What explanation is provided for the eradication of post-secondary education from prisons? Do you agree with these arguments? Why or why not?

16. Black Radical Congress, *1998*
 a. What types of activists are involved in the Black Radical Congress (BRC)?
 b. What documents inspired the BRC's Freedom Agenda and what does this indicate about its political agenda?
 c. What problems within the Black Freedom movement does the BRC's Principles of Unity seek to address?
 d. Do you agree with the Freedom Agenda's statement regarding the conditions to which people are entitled? Why or why not?
17. 2000 Presidential Election
 a. Who were the candidates in the 2000 Presidential Election?
 b. What is the controversy surrounding the votes? Discuss the event that occurred?
 c. Who does Chairperson Mary Frances Berry address this letter to?
 d. What does Chairperson Berry think about the legislation of new voting technology? Is it sufficient to address the barriers that prevented qualified voters from exercising the right to vote?
 e. Chairperson Berry points out several problems with the current voting process. Discuss these problems and what she thinks are the next steps.
18. Hip-Hop Activism
 a. What is hip-hop activism? How is it different from hip-hop?
 b. Discuss the demands that the HSAN (Hop Summit Action Network) puts forth? Are these demands relevant in your life? Why or why not?
 c. What is Tookie calling for all gang members to do? Discuss the potential impact of this document on urban communities?

d. Who is the audience for each document? How does this difference influence the message and who is responsible for the change?

19. World Conference against Racism
    a. Where was the conference held? What is the significance of the conference being held in this location? Who attended the conference?
    b. Why do you think conference participants argued that slavery was a "crime against humanity"? What is the significance of this framing?
    c. How has colonialism and global imbalances hindered the African continent and its descendents?
    d. When the authors discuss the "Black Holocausts," what are they referring to?
    e. The authors make several demands on the United Nations and governments. What are these demands in relation to eliminating anti-black racism? What are these demands in relation to restoring Africa?
    f. What actions should Africans and African descendents take?
20. African Americans Respond to Terrorism and War
    a. What lessons can we learn from Representative Barbara Lee's stand?
    b. How did Representative Lee come to her decision? Do you think her vote reflected the "people"? Why or Why not?
    c. What are three most important reasons why Iraq War veterans oppose the war?
    d. What is the monetary impact of the war on domestic programs? What domestic programs do you think these monies could be diverted to?
21. The Cosby vs. Dyson Debate, *2004–2005*
    a. What are the key points of Bill Cosby's arguments?
    b. How does Michael Eric Dyson's argument differ from Cosby's argument?
    c. Name and discuss two structural equalities that Dyson discusses?
    d. Why are structural inequalities more detrimental than individual behaviors?

e. Reflect on the linguistic uses of "Black English" and/or "Ebonics." Is there a relationship between "Black English" and/or "Ebonics" and the coded language used by African Americans in slavery?

22. U.S. Senate Resolution against Lynching, *2005*
    a. The editors suggest that black people are still the victims of "extreme brutality and extra legal terrorism." What events do you think they are referring to?
    b. What are three key historical events that the resolution discusses?
    c. What did the Senate resolve? Discuss the importance of this resolution in fostering human rights abroad.
23. Hurricane Katrina Crisis, *2005*
    a. Where did Hurricane Katrina hit?
    b. Who was most affected by the devastation of Hurricane Katrina?
    c. Why does Malik Rahim argue that the aftermath of "the tsunami" is different from the aftermath of Hurricane Katrina?
    d. Although hurricanes are considered natural causes, why do you think Rahim argues that Hurricane Katrina was a "criminal" act?
24. Barack Obama's Presidential Campaign, *2007–2008*
    a. In his speeches, Barack Obama discusses his family background. Given his success, why is his background significant? What are the ways that his life is similar and different from the lives of many Americans?
    b. What are four areas that Obama thinks the nation must work on?
    c. Discuss Obama's use of "E pluribus unum" (out of many) and unity, in both speeches.
    d. What is Obama's view of Reverend Wright? On the black church?
    e. Why is the legacy of slavery still important to America today? How do you think slavery has shaped the racial politics of America? What does Obama think must happen to move forward in order to form "A More Perfect Union."
    f. Throughout the speech "A More Perfect Union," Obama discusses several historical events. What are those events? What connections does he make between historical events and current events?

g. Why are black, working-class, and middle-class white Americans angry? Do you think your generation shares the same views?
h. In Obama's view, who and what is causing the "middle-class squeeze"?
i. Throughout his speeches, Obama uses personal stories of Americans to illustrate his points. What do you think about this writing style? Do you think it is effective? Why?

ESSAY QUESTIONS

1. In this section, there are several writings by African-American women. How do the experiences that they discuss broaden understanding of the goals of the Black Freedom movement? What are the implications of these experiences for the realization of democracy?
2. Audre Lorde emphasizes the importance of recognizing difference and challenging the notion that difference signifies deviance or inferiority. Has the struggle for freedom been hindered by the insistence on homogeneity and the perception of difference as threatening?
3. In what ways has the criminal justice system influenced changes in the Black Freedom movement?
4. Both West and Asante point to culture as a critical factor to be considered in the plight of black America. Compare and contrast the ways that each author views culture and its role in the problems and solutions facing African Americans.
5. How are the ideologies of integrationism, black nationalism, and transformationalism evidenced in the works in this section? Do they appear to be in conflict? Why or why not?
6. Identify and examine a contemporary social problem that disproportionately impacts African Americans (e.g., poverty, prison industrial complex, teenage pregnancy, failing public schools) from a historical perspective. Trace the roots of both the problem and the activism that has attempted to combat it.
7. Why has voting been important in the development of the United States?

8. Do you think new racial politics have emerged in the twenty-first century? Why or why not? Use documents from this section and previous sections to defend your answer.

SUGGESTED RESEARCH TOPICS

1. Women political prisoners in the United States
2. The rise of the prison-industrial complex
3. The reparations movement
4. U.S. foreign policy in Africa, Latin America, and the Caribbean during the Reagan–Bush administration (1980–1992)
5. The evolution of black feminist thought
6. History of voting rights, including poll taxes, felony disenfranchisement laws, the suffrage movement, the Nineteenth Amendment, and the Voting Rights Act of 1965
7. Community and hip-hop activist organizations
8. Racial politics outside the United States, particularly among people of African descent in Latin America
9. Institutional racism vs. individual racism
10. Nongovernmental organizations outside the United States working on race and racism

CLASSROOM EXERCISES

1. Pair each student with a member of the opposite sex. Have all female students talk to their partner for five minutes, uninterrupted, about their thoughts on and experiences of gender. After the five minutes, have male students do the same. (The order of participation can be switched.) Then, have them remain in pairs and ask each other questions about what was said. Discuss the results of this exercise as a class, paying close attention to how race, ethnicity, class, and sexual orientation affect students' experiences of gender.

2. Have students watch television and read the newspaper for a week and pick out all stories that have to do with someone breaking the law. After a week, students bring in their findings and discuss the ways in which the media portrays crime and criminality and the implications that this has for the struggle for justice, freedom, and equality.
3. Break the students into groups and have each group develop a political platform and a presidential speech that addresses current issues. Each group should share their platform and select one person to deliver the presidential speech. Afterwards, the groups should debate their platforms.
4. Have students bring in "conscious" hip-hop music that addresses social justice issues. Discuss the lyrics and the issues that the artists address.

MEDIA AND INTERNET RESOURCES

Films

The Body of a Poet: A Tribute to Audre Lorde (Fernando, 1995), *Brick by Brick: A Civil Rights Story* (Kavanagh, 2008), *Close Tallulah NOW!* (Corrections Project, 2002), *Color Adjustment* (CA Newsreel, 1991), *Corrections* (Correction Project, 2001), *Critical Resistance to the Prison Industrial Complex* (Video Activist Network, V.A.N.), *Eyes of the Rainbow: Assata Shakur and Oya* (Rolando, Imagines del Caribe, 1997), *Have You Heard From Johannesburg?: Apartheid and the Club of the West* (Field 2008), *I Shall Not Be Removed: The Life of Marlon Riggs* (CA Newsreel, 1994), *Race: The Power of an Illusion* (CA Newsreel, 2003), *Slam* (Levin, 1998), *Trouble the Water* (Lessin & Deal, 2008), *Tulia, Texas* (Herman & Whalen, 2008), *When the Levees Broke: A Requiem in Four Acts* (HBO, Spike Lee, 2006)

Websites

"2000 Presidential Election"
http://www.eagleton.rutgers.edu/e-gov/e-politicalarchive-2000.htm
"African American/Black/Womanist Feminism on the Web"
http://womenst.library.wisc.edu/fc/fcwebafram.htm

"Afrocentricity: Selected Publications"
http://www.library.cornell.edu/africana/guides/afrocentricity.html
"Can't Stop Won't Stop"
http://www.cantstopwontstop.com/power.cfm
"The Corrections Project"
http://correctionsproject.com
"Iraq War Debate—2002/2007"
http://www.lib.umich.edu/govdocs/iraqwar.html
"Lynching in America"
http://www.liu.edu/cwis/cwp/library/african/2000/lynching.htm
"Million Man March: Photographs"
http://photo2.si.edu/mmm/mmm.html
"The Negro Holocaust: Lynching and Race Riots in the United States, 1880–1950"
http://www.yale.edu/ynhti/curriculum/units/1979/2/79.02.04.x.html#h
"The Prison-Industrial Complex"
http://www.theatlantic.com/issues/98dec/prisons.htm
"The Real Costs of Prisons Project"
http://www.realcostofprisons.org
"The Sentencing Project"
http://www.sentencingproject.org

APPENDICES

ADDITIONAL SOURCES FOR RESEARCH AND WRITING

APPENDIX A

THE ROWMAN & LITTLEFIELD GUIDE TO WRITING WITH SOURCES

The material in the appendices was originally published in *The Rowman & Littlefield Guide to Writing with Sources*, written by James P. Davis.

CONTENTS

"TRUTHINESS" AND THE CHALLENGES OF ACADEMIC WRITING

It's getting too difficult to find nonfiction. Perhaps that's a strange claim when nonfiction books and memoirs are enjoying robust sales. Nonfiction documentary films are getting widespread release at neighborhood cineplexes, and nothing boosts a movie's popularity quite like the claim that it's "based on a real story" or "inspired by real events." News programs are proliferating throughout network and cable television, and some of the most popular prime-time shows are "reality-based." The market reveals that the public has an appetite for truth, reality, nonfiction—whatever we choose to call it. Yet much of what passes for truth is clearly something else—doublespeak, propaganda, plagiarism, advertising, public relations, fraud, spin—what Comedy Central's Stephen Colbert calls "truthiness," a claim or position expressed with seeming certainty that is based not on evidence but on little more than the desire for it to be true.

The media are drawing attention to misrepresentations of information, as is evident in the catch phrases and issues of national news stories. We read that the Iraq War was based on "faulty intelligence." We're told there's a "culture of corruption" in Washington. Authors and political figures accuse each other of "rewriting history." With accusations of bribery, fraud, intelligence leaks, election rigging—these are times when conspiracy theories are abundant, when people are highly skeptical of what they're told, when they presume that a degree of deceit is at work in virtually everything they read or watch. Magazines, critics claim, are under the corporate thumb of advertisers who demand "complimentary copy" and "advertorials" before they provide the essential funding for the publications. Newspapers, we're told, offer perspectives biased by the Left or by the Right. Such esteemed newspapers as the *New York Times*, the *Atlanta Journal-Constitution*, *USA Today*, and the *Los Angeles Times* have recently dismissed plagiarists and issued apologies. Internationally acclaimed scientists have fabricated data about such vital topics as stem cell research and cold nuclear fusion. *USA Today* claims, "The Internet is becoming a cesspool of plagiarism" (Jones 3B). James Frey's best-selling, allegedly autobiographical memoir *A Million Little Pieces* fooled Oprah Winfrey and energized debate about how true nonfiction needs to be. Lawsuits over instances of plagiarism in popular music and best-selling books are commonplace. Broadcast and cable news agencies offer programming so attuned to the sensational and the safe that many viewers prefer to view self-described "fake news" programs (like *The Daily Show* and *The Colbert Report*). Syndicated columnist Frank Rich argues that our obsession with "fictional nonfiction" has moved beyond the reality TV shows whose dialogue is scripted in advance by teams of writers: "What's remarkable is how much fictionalization plays a role in almost every national debate." For 2005, the American Dialect Society chose Colbert's "truthiness" as Word of the Year.

We hope that colleges and universities are havens of clarity, integrity, and critical thinking—where standards of reasonable argumentation and ethics guide communities of teachers and students as they test ideas and learn to reach valid conclusions. Of course, colleges have that potential and sometimes attain it. But they haven't been immune to sloppiness and deceit, as we're reminded whenever we read of a college president, dean, or professor who has been accused of plagiarism. In a graduate program at one large university, more than three dozen current and former students have been accused of plagiarizing in their master's theses (Gray). According to a survey of 50,000 students on over 60 campuses, 70 percent of students admit to having cheated, and half confess to "one or more instances of serious cheating on written assignments" (Campbell). Called a "plague" of plagiarism, this widespread academic dishonesty has been blamed on such things as the ease of cutting and pasting from the Internet or even on habits of intellectual theft encouraged by free music downloading on sites like Napster. It's likely that the continual invention of new technologies and types of sources has left students (and even some of their teachers) confused about how to assess, select, and use both published and electronic information.

Given the challenges posed by abundant material of questionable reliability, it's doubly important that you learn how to make the complex choices involved when you're reading, researching, and writing. Reading with a critical eye involves essential intellectual skills, as you assess the relationship of the information you have found to your project, evaluate its credibility and relevance, select the best use of the material, represent it accurately and fairly, and fully and coherently integrate it into your project. You must also acknowledge and cite the sources you have used in a methodical and clear way. Whether you quote them or paraphrase the information you have found; whether they are published books, unsigned articles, or documents found on the Internet; and whether your project is a formal report, a personal essay, or an oral report in a seminar, you must clearly signal that you have employed these resources and learn to cite them in ways that are ethical, precise, rhetorically effective, and consistent with practices established for the field in which you are writing. Learning to read critically and to write responsibly is crucial—not merely to staying out of trouble but to making sense of one's position during a time of truthiness. Consistently practicing the skills discussed in this book will help you to detect misuse of information by others and to write with more confidence and clearer purpose yourself.

DECISIONS TO MAKE

When you wish to use some information you've found or to quote a viewpoint that is expressed in some source, you need to make a number of decisions.

- Do you need to acknowledge the source of your information?
- Should you paraphrase or quote the material?
- If quoting, how much of the passage should you reproduce in your paper?
- How should you introduce and present the material?

- How should you make the transition to the quoted material and then back to your own prose so that your readers will always understand the status of the words they are reading?
- How should you cite electronic and Internet sources?

This book will help you to answer these questions.

PLAGIARISM

The writing skills involved in using quotations or information from sources are basic ones that you must employ in all of your writing. Your ability to use sources ethically and clearly is crucial to your success in every course, in any major you pursue, in whatever profession you choose. Yet college students often lack these basic skills. The purpose of this book is to enable you to incorporate quoted or paraphrased material into your writing in ways that credit the sources you consult for wording or ideas that are not your own and that will permit your audience to comprehend your ideas and to have confidence in your authority as a writer. Mastering the skills discussed here will broaden your options as you write, increase your confidence as a student, and empower you to write with clarity and authority. Neglecting these skills will cripple your abilities to communicate and, worse, in some cases, render you vulnerable to charges of academic dishonesty.

Very few students plan to cheat when they begin a course or when they begin a specific project. Most cases of academic dishonesty arise from poor planning, procrastination, carelessness, or intrusions of stress into students' lives that they haven't learned to manage. As a deadline approaches, they might be tempted to lift ideas or phrases from someone else's work. Or, in a rush to complete a project, they allow themselves to take such sloppy notes that they can no longer tell what is their phrasing or what is someone else's or which source might have provided something that is scrawled in their notebook. In an English class, they might feel they can use unacknowledged ideas from *Cliff's* notes or Sparknotes.com. Students usually realize that these are such undistinguished study guides that they don't want to disclose they've consulted them—but some of the wording or an occasional idea might seem too good not to use in an essay. Even if students don't think they are doing anything wrong, even if the idea or phrase trickled into their work through carelessness or haste, these violations are taken as seriously as if students copied someone else's lab report or put their name on an essay written by someone else. You shouldn't consult a source that you would be ashamed to cite. If you ever have a question about the way you are completing an assignment, ask your professor or lab assistant how to proceed. For example, although most instructors will not allow you to submit an essay written during a prior semester for a different class, it might be possible to combine two projects from different classes into one—but only if both professors are fully aware of and approve of what you're doing.

The Web has produced its own set of temptations to students. It might not seem like cheating when all one has to do is point and click to find some ready-made phrasing, without even needing to transcribe it. Students might genuinely believe, if they find some information or phrasing on more than one website, that it must be common knowledge or public property—forgetting that the websites themselves might have plagiarized from each other or some third source. But using any idea or information that is not common knowledge without carefully and properly acknowledging that you've done so is a form of serious academic dishonesty that—students are often surprised to learn—instructors detect easily. Instructors are familiar with the capabilities of most students and sensitive to features of individual students' writing styles. They are also familiar with the published work in their fields, well trained to recognize the contributions and stylistic habits of professional writers. A variety of specialized search engines and online services enable instructors to locate the original sources of wording and ideas stolen from published and electronic sources, often more quickly than the student was able to find it in the first place.

Plagiarism has never been so easy—but it has never been so easy to detect. No one enjoys being suspicious, and no task is more abhorrent to an instructor than confronting a dishonest or careless student and proceeding with judicial action. It is far more satisfying to work with students to train them to use sources responsibly before questions of their integrity arise. You must do your part to make certain that you understand this material and apply it whenever you write a paper. Don't let the fear of misusing quoted material dissuade you from doing research. Instead, master the skills of quoting and paraphrasing responsibly, confident that, when you do so, you will gain a powerful and indispensable skill.

POPULAR STYLE MANUALS

Different disciplines follow different conventions for citing sources used in a project. Students might view these differences as unimportant, as if the rules are arbitrary or result from instructor preference. But formats for citing materials are not random. They have been designed by professional organizations to present citations in systematic ways that reflect the priorities and core values of that field. A book or pamphlet that presents a specific format is called a style manual. If an instructor has not specified which style manual to follow, it is a student's responsibility to ask which one to use and to follow its guidelines for formatting and printing the document and, most important, for how to arrange footnotes, endnotes, and a list of works cited. Most style manuals are available in your college or public library, and many are online. It's a good idea, once you have declared a major or begun graduate work within a particular field, to purchase a current copy of the style manual for that field. Some commonly used style manuals include the following:

1. Modern Language Association's *MLA Handbook for Writers of Research Papers*, for English and modern languages
2. Turabian's *Manual for Writers of Term Papers, Theses, and Dissertations*, for history and other humanities (based on the *Chicago Manual of Style*)
3. *Scientific Style and Format*, published by the Council of Science Editors (CSE), for biological sciences
4. *Publication Manual of the American Psychological Association* (APA) for psychology
5. *Handbook for Authors*, published by the American Chemical Society, for chemistry
6. *Style Manual for Political Science*, published by the American Political Science Association (APSA), for political science

This book does not present comprehensive citation formats for all fields. Because my discipline is English, my own citations will follow the format presented in the *MLA Handbook.* Whatever style manual you use for a particular course or paper, remember that the purpose of all of them is threefold:

1. To help you establish your authority and provide documentation for your claims in a systematic way
2. To help you provide your readers with all of the information they need to find your original sources and verify your claims about them
3. To provide a system for briefly identifying a source in your text with minimum textual clutter in ways that clearly refer to the fully cited work in a list at the end

ELEMENTS REQUIRED IN A CITATION

Before you begin to gather information and take notes for a project, you need to know what sorts of information about the source you need to cite it properly—both in your list of works cited and in those portions of your text where you have used it.

If you are taking information from a book, all style sheets demand that you include in the final list:

- author
- title
- volume number (if a multivolume work)
- date of publication
- place of publication
- publisher
- page number(s)

Within your text itself, you may need to provide only the author's last name and a page number (or, for some disciplines, a year of publication). If you have used only one work by that author, it will be clear to which work in the list the name refers.

For articles, your works cited list must include:

- author
- title of the article
- title of the journal or magazine
- volume and issue numbers
- date
- page number(s)

As you do with books, in your text itself you should keep your information about a source as brief as you can, providing just enough information to enable your reader to identify the full citation in your list at the end. You refer to the full citation with the author's name (if known) or with an abbreviated title of the article (if the author is not known), and the page number.

Internet sources may or may not name their authors, and they won't have conventional page numbers. While you still have the source before you, you might need to go the home page or follow some other link to find out when the site was most recently revised and to find out the name of the author or sponsoring organization. If a website does not indicate a person or organization that is responsible for it, you will probably not find it to be reputable enough to be worth consulting. When this information is available, you will need to provide the name of the author or organization and the title of the site (probably abbreviated for your in-text references). Make certain that you provide in your list of works cited the entire electronic address (or URL). Because an electronic source is likely to change frequently, it's also crucial that you provide the date you consulted it.

When you take notes, make sure that you distinguish carefully between quoted words and your own words, and note the page number of print sources from which the information was taken. Copy all of the necessary information (as specified above) that would allow someone else to locate that source. Spare yourself the need to return to the library simply to find the name of the publisher or the page number from which a certain quotation or paraphrased information came. *One further caution*: it is not adequate merely to list a work you have used in your works cited. You must at all times make certain that it is clear what portion of your work has used what portion of the cited source.

Following sections of this book present ways to select and incorporate material into your work that are shared by all disciplines. Get into the habit now of employing the following suggestions. You will find that all of your writing will be stronger.

WHEN DO YOU NEED TO ACKNOWLEDGE A SOURCE?

Some of what you write will come from your own observations and experience, some from class notes and discussion, some from what we call "common knowledge," some from the assigned readings in the course, some from works you've sought out on your own. Each of these sources merits a bit of discussion.

Obviously, you need not document in any formal way your own observations or experiences. The power of your own written voice should convince your readers of the plausibility of your own ideas and experiences.

MATERIAL FROM CLASSROOM DISCUSSION

In most circumstances, you are free to incorporate ideas that have been explored in class discussion without worrying about the ownership of those ideas. Usually you may feel free to draw on background information presented in class as you provide a context for the more focused and developed discussion in your paper. If the class lecture or discussion itself has drawn on sources, such as films or readings, then you should attribute relevant ideas to their original source. But instructors do not expect or desire credit in your paper for ideas generated in class. Two suggestions:

1. Your own paper should probably not consist entirely of ideas repeated from class. Instead, it should develop ideas more fully or apply them in new ways that demonstrate your understanding of them. Ask your instructor for suggestions, if you are concerned that your paper may simply rehash ideas presented in class.
2. When you do rely on ideas or information from class, remember to explain them fully. Unless your professor specifies a particular kind of audience for your project, think of your reader as a person who is intelligent but who has not attended class. Anyone who picks up your paper should be able to understand it—not just the professor for whom you have written the paper.

COMMON KNOWLEDGE

The category of information we call "common knowledge" is a more complex matter. Common knowledge includes broad historical facts that are not the conclusions or discoveries of a particular author, for example the fact that John Kennedy was the thirty-fifth president of the United States, or that Emily Brontë died the year after *Wuthering Heights* was published, or that under normal atmospheric pressure, water boils at 100 degrees Celsius. Even if you have to look up common-knowledge facts like these in a reference work, you do not need to cite your source. Nor do you have to document commonly known generalizations, such as the assumption that the Romantic Era in British literature was a time of intense literary innovation, or that computers have revolutionized communication, or that laboratory experimentation with animals is controversial. When you are beginning your studies of a particular subject, you might not always be able to tell easily what is common knowledge within a discipline and what isn't. But as you read more widely in a field with an eye toward what the other authors assume is shared information, you will be better able to assess what information properly belongs to particular authors. Two cautions:

1. Even if you judge a bit of information to be shared publicly, be careful not to represent another writer's phrasing of this common knowledge

as your own. Although the information may be common knowledge, a specific writer's expression of the information is still the property of that writer.

2. If you cannot decide if some information needs to be credited to an author, provide a reference giving such credit. When in doubt, cite your source.

Common knowledge also includes traditional tales, folk literature, and folk wisdom—tales or observations that are handed down without the knowledge of who wrote the tale or made the observation. Many fairy tales—for instance those of Mother Goose—or age-old songs and jokes—such as "Three Blind Mice" and "Why did the chicken cross the road?"—do not require documentation of the source. Nor would you need to provide a note crediting some source with the observation that a dog is a man's best friend, that absence makes the heart grow fonder, or that a bird in the hand is worth two in the bush. Many clichés or sayings fall into this category, though where authors are known, you should mention them. You should, for example, acknowledge that it was Alexander Pope who wrote "To err is human, to forgive divine," or Thomas Paine who wrote "These are the times that try men's souls." But generalized, commonsense observations do not usually need to be credited to a source. Be forewarned, however, that most readers will not continue reading something that tells them things they already know, and they will probably be irritated if your phrasing is hackneyed or your observations trite. If you use clichés in formal writing, use them in some fresh or unexpected way, or your readers will probably assume that you have nothing new to say and may lose interest in what you've written.

USING TEXTBOOKS AS SOURCES

When you draw on information from a course textbook or from a source you have found on your own, you need to credit the source for all information drawn from it that is not common knowledge. For informal papers in which you refer only to class textbooks, professors may not demand that you give a complete reference that includes all of the publication facts. Ask your professor if it is acceptable merely to specify the author and title and put the page number from which the information was taken in parentheses at the end of the sentence. Even if the source is a class textbook and the author and title are clear from the context (the assignment is a paper on *Wuthering Heights*, for example), you must at least cite the edition and page number because your professor will want to be able to locate the exact page from which you are getting the information, whether you quote it directly or paraphrase it. Even when you are writing a short "homework" or in-class assignment, you should acknowledge material that is not your own. You should provide proper citations of your sources not merely to avoid plagiarism, but to empower your writing with authority, evidence, and illustrative detail.

Remember to acknowledge the source of any visual material you've included in your essay, unless that material is truly in public domain or is provided by your word processing program as clip art. For example, if you incorporate photographs or drawings in your written project (and you did not create them), you must acknowledge the source of this material. A brief reference in a caption for the picture, followed by a full citation in your list of works cited, will usually suffice for class assignments.

USING SOURCES IN CLASS PRESENTATIONS

In the give and take of ordinary class discussion, no one expects or desires attention to source material beyond mentioning an author's name or, at most, a page number of a book if others have copies of it with them. But a report to the class is a different matter. The more formal, lengthy, and public the presentation, the more thoroughly you should acknowledge the sources you've used.

If your report is entirely verbal (without use of PowerPoint or other visual material), acknowledge your use of information that is not common knowledge by referring to the name of the author of a publication as you present the information from that source. At the end of your talk, you can offer to share a printed list of the works you cite, a list that you should put in the proper format for the discipline. Such a practice doesn't add to the length of your talk, nor does it add any tedium or clutter. It demonstrates your care about ownership of ideas, and it adds to the authority of your comments by noting the studies you have consulted. Offering to share the citations list shows your respect not only for the published authors but for the other students in the course, as well.

If you are augmenting your presentation with PowerPoint, the visual text gives you a ready place to acknowledge source material. The PowerPoint text should not exactly duplicate what you are saying, or the effect will be redundant and tedious to your audience. You might signal the architecture of your talk with an outline, but you should resist the impulse to project your text as you speak it. In general, reserve the images you include for things that are best presented visually. You might want to display an important quotation that you're planning to discuss, and such a passage should include a citation of its source. You might use a diagram that illustrates relationships among the things you are discussing. If you use a diagram that you've found in print or on the Web, be certain to provide a full citation for it.

Whenever you include graphic materials, be very careful to assess the degree to which they are protected by copyright laws. Of course, you may use clip art as freely as you might any of the graphics enhancements that come with the software you're using. But if you include a photograph or a film or audio clip, you must acknowledge the proper source for the material. That source is probably not the search engine you employed to find it. For example, if you wanted an image of garment industry workers, you could conduct an image search on Google to find a wide assortment of images. If you choose one to use, the proper source to cite would not be Google—it would be the website that Google alerted you to. You should go to that site to find the name of the author or sponsoring organization, the title of the site, the URL and so forth. The same would be true for film clips or sound recordings that you are incorporating into your presentation. Make certain to find all of the information required for a full citation of the actual source, and include that citation (probably in a modestly sized font) on the screen during your presentation. Showing such care is important in establishing the authenticity of the materials you're including and in avoiding improper or unethical uses of published material. If you're using images, photos, and clips to complete a class project, make sure you acknowledge the proper source in proper form. In these circumstances, with this limited purpose and with proper citation, the law generally grants you this "fair use" of the material.

If your presentation is going to be posted on a course webpage or in any other way made available on the Internet, your use of such materials without proper citation could involve more than academic dishonesty. It could involve legal matters of violated copyright. Using such copyrighted material for purposes other than completion of an assignment for a class might require you to pay permissions fees and use specific language in your acknowledgments. Public and for-profit use of copyrighted tables, charts, poems, songs, film clips, sound recordings, and photographs nearly always requires written permission from the owner of the text.

WHEN SHOULD YOU PARAPHRASE AND WHEN SHOULD YOU QUOTE?

Done properly, paraphrasing information gives you remarkable flexibility and, by permitting you to select only the information most relevant to your topic, it enables you to express your ideas with a minimum of verbiage. In short, it ensures that all of the information is pertinent, and it helps you to write with economy and vigor. When readers encounter information paraphrased or summarized from one of your sources, they do not have to move between writing by you and that by another author, shifting to a new voice, a new style, a different pace and context. When you paraphrase well, you do your reader a great service, because you've selected, organized, and phrased the information to suit your purposes, all in a manner that preserves a continuity of style and emphasis. But paraphrasing requires more work of you than simply copying someone else's words.

It is appropriate for you to paraphrase, instead of quoting, whenever the wording itself is less important to the purpose of your writing than the information it presents. If all you need from an economic study, for example, is the distressing information that, nationally, a woman with a college degree has the same earning potential as a male high school dropout, simply paraphrase the conclusions of the study in your own words and state your source, rather than quoting the study. Citing a statistic, a relatively unknown fact, a bit of information embedded in a study that otherwise is not relevant to your topic—in all of these situations, it is advisable to paraphrase rather than to quote.

Conversely, if the source itself is important to your topic, if the original wording helps you to illustrate your point, if the opinion expressed in the passage is controversial or highly unusual, or if the work itself *is* your subject (as in a paper on a literary work or an analysis of a text), then it is advisable to quote the actual words the original author used.

The next time you watch a televised news program, notice how the news writers use sources to establish the credibility of their reporting. The orchestrated movements to and from different locations, to and from other correspondents, other cameras and voices—these movements are analogous to an author's presentation of information in nonfiction writing. If they chose to, news anchors could present all of the news stories in their (or their news editor's) own words. Actually, doing so would provide better quality of both visual images and recorded language than the grainy, sometimes poorly focused film footage that is shot by foreign correspondents with their hand-held cameras in the heat of battle. Many news anchors do present much of the information themselves, particularly economic news (which doesn't film very dramatically) or stories for which they have no taped footage. But roughly half of the time, they turn the story over to a person in the field, to an eyewitness speaking without revising, or to a correspondent who narrates over some film footage, blurred by the processes of photography, distanced by the satellite transmission. Why? The answer is probably obvious. Going to the sources that are close to the story, to the people who are more authoritative than are the anchors themselves, contributes to their credibility. The news anchors become more authoritative for knowing when to let someone else be the authority. They introduce the news item and the taped footage, they let us know who is speaking, then they show us a tape, frequently following the segment with some kind of concluding remarks to give the story a sense of closure. Any edition of the evening news will demonstrate a similar use of primary source material. Even though the conventions of video documentation differ from those of printed writing—for example, there are no footnotes in a newscast—the purpose of such material is evident.

Paraphrase (with proper citations) when all you need is the information itself.

Quote when your source is important, when you can gain authority by turning to another author.

HOW SHOULD YOU PARAPHRASE INFORMATION FROM A SOURCE?

Once you've decided that the occasion calls for paraphrasing, you need to do several things.

SELECTING INFORMATION FROM YOUR SOURCE

First, you need to select the information relevant to your topic and make certain that you completely rephrase the ideas—in your own words. Do not use any phrases, syntax, or organization that appeared in the original work. These are the author's personal property, and representing segments or features of a passage as your own constitutes plagiarism.

An Example of Paraphrasing

Suppose you are writing a paper on blue jeans as a cultural phenomenon, exploring what the enduring popularity of blue jeans illustrates about our culture. You find an essay in *American Heritage*, "The Jeaning of America—and the World," by Carin Quinn, in which she writes the following about Levi's jeans (on page 18):

> The pants have become a tradition, and along the way have acquired a history of their own—so much so that the company has opened a museum in San

> Francisco. There was, for example, the turn-of-the-century trainman who replaced a faulty coupling with a pair of jeans; the Wyoming man who used his jeans as a towrope to haul his car out of a ditch; the Californian who found several pairs in an abandoned mine, wore them, then discovered they were sixty-three years old and still as good as new and turned them over to the Smithsonian as a tribute to their toughness. And then there is the particularly terrifying story of the careless construction worker who dangled fifty-two stories above the street until rescued, his sole support the Levi's belt loop through which his rope was hooked.

You decide that the information about the museum and Quinn's examples of heroically strong jeans would strengthen your argument about what the jeans symbolize, and you write the following:

> The jeans have earned a history all their own—to such an extent that the Levi's corporation even operates a museum of jeans in San Francisco. The museum presents the stories of the trainman who hitched two trains together with a pair of jeans, of the Wyoming man who towed his car out of ditch using a pair of the jeans, of the Californian who found several pairs in an abandoned mine, put them on, discovered they were still good as new after sixty-three years, and donated them to the Smithsonian as a tribute to their toughness. One especially horrifying story is that of the construction worker who lost his footing and dangled some fifty stories over the street, hanging only from the Levi's belt loop which his rope was hooked on. [improper paraphrase—plagiarism]

If you left this paragraph in your paper—even if you provided a note naming Carin Quinn as your source, and even if you didn't intend to deceive anyone—you would be guilty of plagiarism. Even though much of the paragraph has been rephrased, much of it hasn't been. This paragraph is organized exactly like the original, and much of the rewriting is merely substitution of synonyms for her original words, relying far too heavily on her syntax. The phrase "particularly terrifying," for example, is replaced by "especially horrifying," with much of the original sentence left intact. The exact repetition of "found several pairs in an abandoned mine" and of the phrase "tribute to their toughness" is especially damning. If this wording is important enough to repeat verbatim, then you should quote it; otherwise, the passage should be completely reworded.

A far better example of paraphrasing, one that incorporates Quinn's ideas into the author's own argument, would be the following use of the material:

> Every morning, as you slip into your jeans, you put on a part of American history. You might merely be seeking warmth on a cold day or trying to make yourself decent for a walk downtown, but your jeans bring with them a long cultural tradition and probably more legendary strength than you'll ever need to run your errands. According to Carin Quinn, a pair of the original Levi's served once as a rope for a man in Wyoming who needed to tow his car from a ditch. A trainman once used a pair of the jeans to couple together two railway cars when the original coupling had broken. And when a hapless construction worker lost his footing fifty-two stories above the earth, one loop of his jeans was sufficient to hold him until help arrived (18). The Levi's corporation is well aware of its image. The leather patch with the Levi trademark shows a pair of jeans pulled between two horses. Most days you probably won't be repairing trains, dangling overhead, or deliberately frustrating the movement of horses, but wearing blue jeans symbolically connects you with the strength, ingenuity, preparedness, and even heroism embodied in these legends about the jeans.

Granted, this paragraph contains many ideas not found in the original source. And Quinn's paragraph presents information not included in this passage. But that's part of the point. You shouldn't simply repeat ideas you've found elsewhere; you should incorporate those ideas into a context all your own. And you should make clear which of the ideas in the paragraph derive from Quinn's work and which are entirely your own. Including the author's name at the beginning and a page or note number (depending on your style sheet) at the end of the paraphrased material makes it clear which information came from the source and which didn't. When you do find some useful information in a source you've consulted, you should explicitly name the author, select only those details that suit your purpose, phrase them in wording that is entirely your own, provide the page number, and then print the full publishing information in a list of works cited at the end of your paper.

GIVING CREDIT TO YOUR SOURCE

The second thing you must do has already been mentioned but bears repeating here: Even if you are not quoting actual words, you need to give credit for the information, and you need to make clear exactly what has come from your source. Sometimes students believe that all they need to do if they've drawn information from a source is provide the author's name in parentheses (or a note number) at the end of the paragraph containing the paraphrased material, confident that they've given credit where credit is due. This practice, however, is dangerously ambiguous and even misleading. A citation at the end of a paragraph implies that *all* of the material in the paragraph had its origin in the cited source, even if the paragraph is a mix of borrowed information and original insight. This practice might attribute ideas to the cited author that he or she did not develop, and it completely muddies the distinction between your own ideas and the author's. For example, in the last sample paragraph on jeans, if I had not mentioned the author's name where I did and if I had waited until the end of the paragraph to provide the page (or note) number, I would have inaccurately represented all of the ideas in the paragraph as Quinn's, thereby denying myself credit for the ideas that precede and follow the paraphrased material. Quinn does not make the observation that Levi's represents American ingenuity and preparedness for adversity. That idea is mine, and I shouldn't allow mere sloppiness with writing technique to rob me of credit for the discovery. The author's name at the beginning of the paraphrased material and the page number at the end of it function a bit as the beginning and ending quotation marks would if the material were quoted—they set off the cited information from your own, signaling its different status from the other words, identifying the source with maximum clarity and minimal distraction. In short, think of embedding the paraphrased material in your own prose as a kind of linguistic bracketing or fencing off of the information in as clear a way as possible, so as not to give the author too little credit—or too much.

THE IMPORTANCE OF ACCURACY IN PARAPHRASING

Finally, you need to make certain that your synopsis of the author's ideas accurately reflects the author's actual statement. It probably goes without saying that you shouldn't misrepresent a paraphrased source, yet often students seem rather cavalier about restating others' ideas. Notice how frequently letters to the editor in your newspaper attempt to correct a perceived misreading or misrepresentation of an earlier letter. In the heat of the debate about social or political issues, people often say things imprecisely and misread the letters of others. Most of your sources are far more carefully composed than such letters. So should be your reading of them. Imagine that the authors whose words you are paraphrasing are going to read your synopsis of what they said. Will they feel that their views have been accurately and fairly represented? You may certainly disagree with what an author says in print, but it only helps to establish your credibility if you present those ideas fairly (maybe even quoting especially pertinent lines), before going on to demonstrate what is wrong with the author's position.

The focus and length of your project should guide you as you decide how much of the source you plan to use. It is usually best not to use only a general or concluding remark as if it is sufficient by itself to constitute evidence or argument. Neglecting to explain the author's reasons for her or his position and simply using a general phrase from the work will make it seem as if you are content to rely on authority assertions rather than to critically assess the ideas. Whether you agree with or challenge the published view (paraphrased or quoted), it helps you to establish your thoroughness and fairness if you attend to the reasoning behind an author's conclusions as you use the material.

HOW SHOULD YOU QUOTE MATERIAL FROM A SOURCE?

HOW MUCH TO QUOTE

Students sometimes wonder what proportion of their papers should be quoted material and what should be original words of their own. At one extreme, their papers might consist of lengthy quoted passages, stitched together with a few transitions of their own, as if writing is like assembling a patchwork quilt out of fragments of others' cloth. At the other extreme, students might quote only once, leaving most of their paragraphs without quotations to serve as illustration or evidence. Either extreme is disproportionate. Think of quoting as a valuable means of developing and supporting ideas—not as the means of presenting the ideas themselves. In some cases, quotations will be the best form your evidence could take, and neglecting to include relevant quotations could mean neglecting to provide convincing illustrative material. When you are revising your paper, read through it once without reading the quoted words. If your paper makes little sense without the quotations, you've probably attempted to make them do too much. Your words should present your argument; the quotations are only supportive material—valuable and essential to convincing your reader but never the primary means of presenting information.

HOW TO PRESENT A QUOTATION

Once you've decided that it is appropriate to quote, you need to decide how much of the passage merits being presented in your paper. It may be that the information you need is entangled in a long sentence or paragraph, most of which is beside your immediate point. In this case, were you to quote the entire sentence or paragraph, you would needlessly divert your reader's attention from your immediate topic. You can quote passages of virtually any length: a word, a phrase, a sentence, even a paragraph. But whatever you quote should be entirely relevant to your purpose, and the longer the passage you quote, the greater should be your use of the material. Most of the time it would be rhetorically ineffective to quote a long passage, unless you plan to analyze or interpret it at some length, following the quotation. In most instances, your task will be to select a phrase or sentence that best illustrates the point you are making, and, taking great care to copy the material exactly as it is written, fit the quoted author's words into your own, making certain that you mark the quoted passage with quotation marks, name the source of the material (if it isn't already clear in the paragraph), and work the phrases into your own in a way that produces grammatical and coherent statements. If you fit a quoted phrase into a sentence, check for two things:

1. Between the opening and closing quotation marks, every symbol should be reproduced exactly at it appears in the original, unless you've clearly indicated what changes you made in the ways explained below.
2. Try reading your paragraph as if there were no quotation marks present. All of the words, quoted and unquoted, must function together in grammatical and coherent ways.

Never present a quotation as a completely separate sentence. Always introduce it in some way. The presence of quotation marks (without any introduction or transition) is not a sufficient signal that the material has come from a source, because writers use quotation marks for some purposes other than quoting. They might mark a word that they are using in a special way or mark a word that they are discussing. When I mentioned "common knowledge" above, I put it in quotation marks, because I was discussing what the phrase means. Some authors who need to use a slang expression will surround the expression with quotation marks as if to apologize for using the phrase. It is not a particularly admirable practice, but it is a fairly common one. Don't "fly off the handle" at such practices; instead, keep your "cool." The important point here is to introduce all quotations in ways that indicate you are quoting, that identify the source, and that suggest the significance of what the person is saying.

As you lead into a quoted passage, you should consider what sorts of information about your source the reader needs to know to understand the significance of the quotation.

- Does the author have a position or credentials that are relevant to the quoted statement?
- Is the date of the statement important enough to note as you introduce it?
- Was the quoted passage published originally as a part of a major study?
- Has the author employed a particular research methodology that might contextualize the study within the field?
- Has the author made use of important or unusual materials?
- Is the journal or other medium in which the piece appears particularly noteworthy?

If you know this kind of information and it helps to establish the context of the material within the field of your topic, you should consider including it as you introduce a quoted passage. Think of the reasons that you consulted the source in the first place and the reasons why you selected the passage that you did.

If you can signal these reasons to your reader as you introduce the material, your reader might better understand the relationship of the quoted passage to your essay. At the very least, you should convey that the quoted material comes from a source:

"According to one study . . . "
"One author puts it this way . . . "
"A later report claims that . . . "

Better yet, name the source:

> "Miller argues that . . . "
> "Johnston, who studied the mosquito for fifteen years, postulates that . . . "
> "The chief engineer on the project, Eliza Swaney, observes . . . "

And if the passage is important, alert your reader to the nature of its significance or to its context in your work:

> "Jonathan Alder offers a contrasting view . . . "
> "Linkholder's rebuttal shows her dependence on Connelly's theorem . . . "
> "Note the veiled anger in Cramer's reply . . . "

Your objective is to signal your movements to and from a quotation with maximum clarity, continuity, and context, and to encourage your reader to predict what will follow in a quotation. As you read authors you admire in the field for which you are writing, get in the habit of noticing how the authors have chosen to do what they do. When you encounter writing done well, read it carefully, not just for the information you need, but to learn from the example alternate ways of meeting your needs as a writer.

HOW TO SHOW ADDITIONS AND DELETIONS IN A QUOTATION

Between the opening set of quotation marks and the closing pair, every word, letter, and punctuation mark must be exactly as it appears in the original. You can change some of the things in a quotation—adding or deleting words—but only if you indicate that you have done so and only if your change does not distort the meaning of what you've quoted. One change is permitted—actually required—within a quotation: If the source itself quotes something else, you change the double quotation marks to single ones, so that they are not confused with the ones that you have provided. You may also change the final punctuation mark in your quotation of a passage to suit your own grammatical needs (see below), in effect stopping your quoting before the final symbol. But if grammar demands that you add a word, change the tense of a quoted verb, or clarify the reference of a quoted pronoun, for instance, you should do so by enclosing your change in square brackets (not parentheses). If you are using a typewriter and it does not have square brackets, [or], leave spaces as you type where the brackets should be and write them in neatly in black ink.

If for reasons of clarity, grammar, or brevity, you decide to delete a word or phrase from within a series of quoted words, put in its place an ellipsis, three spaced dots . . . , to show your reader that you've left something out. If you are quoting a passage that itself already makes use of an ellipsis, place the periods you add within square brackets to distinguish between those you added to show your deletion and those already in the text you quote. In this situation, you should space once before the opening bracket, *between* the periods themselves, and once after the closing bracket, so that your ellipsis looks like this: [. . .] If the passage you are quoting does not already make use of an ellipsis, simply add the required periods without the brackets. If quoting the passage requires extensive bracketing and ellipses, to the extent that you must undergo all sorts of grammatical or typographic contortions, consider paraphrasing the material or quoting only the most relevant phrases or words. The following examples will illustrate how to use square brackets and the ellipsis.

Assume for the moment that you are writing an essay on Fitzgerald's *The Great Gatsby*, exploring the ways in which the narrator, Nick Carraway, is biased as he relates the events. Because your topic is a work of literature, and especially because you are attempting to show how the narrator's language reveals his attitudes, you will frequently wish to quote from the novel. You will find no more direct source of evidence to convince skeptical readers than quoting the actual novel.

Using Square Brackets to Mark Words Added to a Quotation

Original (from page 39 of Fitzgerald's *The Great Gatsby*):
In his blue gardens men and girls came and went like moths among the whisperings and the champagne and the stars.

Your use of the passage (the page number follows the passage):
Nick Carraway, the narrator in the novel, says that "In his [Gatsby's] blue

> gardens men and girls came and went like moths among the whisperings and the champagne and the stars" (39).

Explanation

By itself, the original "his" in the passage would have incorrectly implied that the gardens under discussion were Nick's instead of Gatsby's. In this case, a more graceful way of clarifying the meaning of the pronoun would be to provide a referent for "his" as you introduce the quotation, as in the following:

> Early in the novel, Nick reveals his contempt for Gatsby's guests: "In his blue gardens men and girls came and went like moths among the whisperings and the champagne and the stars" (39).

This use of the material avoids the clutter of the brackets and better alerts the reader to notice Nick's judgment of the guests. Yet another way to use this material (and other relevant details from the novel) might be to write the following:

> Despite Nick's early claim that he is "inclined to reserve all judgments" (1), he says that Tom has "a cruel body" (7), and he refers to Gatsby's guests as "moths" (39).

This might be an even better use of the material, depending on the focus and context of the essay. It explains why it matters that Nick is in fact judgmental, and it makes use of selected phrases or words that illustrate this trait. Within the pairs of quotation marks, every word is identical to the original. And each quotation is followed by the number of the page on which the passage appears. If you can rework your use of a passage to avoid using the brackets, do so. But if you need to change something, employ the brackets to signify that change. Following is one more example of how bracketed information may clarify the meaning of a pronoun. While it is clear in the novel that Nick is speaking of Gatsby in these lines, removing the passage from its context requires that you clarify the meaning in your context.

> **Original** (from page 102):
> For several weeks I didn't see him or hear his voice on the phone—mostly I was in New York, trotting around with Jordan and trying to ingratiate

myself with her senile aunt—but finally I went over to his house one Sunday afternoon.

Your use of the material:
Nick makes it clear that the only events of that summer that interest him now are those involving Gatsby. At one point he alludes to other events, but he quickly returns to his real subject:

> For several weeks I didn't see him [Gatsby] or hear his voice on the phone—mostly I was in New York, trotting around with Jordan and trying to ingratiate myself with her senile aunt—but finally I went over to his house one Sunday afternoon. (102)

Here Nick summarizes "several weeks" in only nineteen words, those weeks not mattering because they didn't involve his hero, Gatsby.

Explanation

Notice again the simple way you can clear up a potentially confusing pronoun with information enclosed in brackets. Notice also that, when the quoted passage is relatively long (more than three typed lines), you present it in "block" format: you set it off from the rest of your text by indenting it. When you present block quotations, you should not enclose the material in quotation marks unless they appear in the original. Setting it off in block format already tells the reader that the material is quoted. The page number or any other parenthetical publication information follows the period in a block quotation. Notice also that the paragraph does not end simply because I presented a block quotation. I followed the passage with attention to its details, connecting it to the idea I'm developing. Beginning and closing lines in paragraphs are positions of extreme emphasis; don't leave your reader dangling at the end of block quotations. Resume your analysis, closing the paragraph by returning to your immediate point.

If your paper is written in the present tense and you wish to quote something written in the past tense, bracket the part of the verb you change:

Original (from page 80):
He had waited five years and bought a mansion where he dispensed starlight to casual moths—so that he could "come over" some afternoon to a stranger's garden.

Your use of the material:
Nick implies throughout the novel that Gatsby's guests are undeserving of his social efforts, saying that Gatsby "dispense[s] starlight to casual moths" (80).

Notice, as always, the quoted material is introduced in some way that makes its source and its importance clear to your reader.

Using the Ellipsis to Indicate That You Deleted Words from a Quotation

If you decide, in the interests of brevity and relevance, to leave out some material from within a quoted passage, provide the ellipsis (three spaced periods) to show it. The deletion, obviously, should not change the meaning of the passage, nor should it produce a series of words that do not fit grammatically with the rest of your writing. If you are omitting an entire sentence or more from within a quotation, you should provide the regular period at the end of the sentence before the deleted material, and then provide the usual ellipsis (three spaced periods) to show that one or more sentences have been deleted. Do not begin or end a quotation with ellipses, especially if you are quoting only a word or a phrase. Surrounding the quoted material with ellipses only adds unnecessary clutter. If the passage itself already contains an ellipsis, place the ellipsis within square brackets. The brackets will enable your reader to distinguish between the ellipsis you have added and the spaced periods used for some other purpose by the author of the original passage.

Suppose you are writing an essay on the psychology behind the marketing of sport utility vehicles. You find an essay by Malcolm Gladwell called "Big and Bad: How the S.U.V. Ran Over Automotive Safety" (*New Yorker*, 12 January 2004). Because Gladwell incorporates in his essay various studies and interviews with automotive marketing specialists, you decide to use some of the material from the following passage:

Original (from page 31):
The S.U.V. boom represents, then, a shift in how we conceive of safety—from active to passive. It's what happens when a larger number of drivers

conclude, consciously or otherwise, that the extra thirty feet that the Trail-Blazer takes to come to a stop doesn't really matter, that the tractor-trailer will hit them anyway, and that they are better off treating accidents as inevitable rather than avoidable. "The metric that people use is size," says Stephen Popiel, a vice-president of Millward Brown Goldfarb, in Toronto, one of the leading automotive market-research firms. "The bigger something is, the safer it is. In the consumer's mind, the basic equation is, If I were to take this vehicle and drive it into this brick wall, the more metal there is in front of me the better off I'll be."

Your use of the material:
One of the reasons that S.U.V.s are so profitable to manufacture is that, classified as trucks, they need not meet government safety standards established for passenger cars. Yet nearly all of the advertisements for S.U.V.s promote safety as the vehicles' chief advantage. Seated far from the road, surrounded by massive expanses of cushioned plastic and many of the amenities of home, drivers of S.U.V.s certainly *feel* safe, despite the loss of maneuverability and braking power as the size and weight of vehicles increase. "The S.U.V. boom," according to Malcolm Gladwell, "represents . . . a shift in how [American drivers] conceive of safety—from active to passive." A passive view of safety reflects a general assumption that people don't have much control over what happens to them, so they should be prepared for the worst and treat "accidents as inevitable rather than avoidable." Gladwell quotes market-researcher Stephen Popiel: "The metric that people use is size. . . . The bigger something is, the safer it is" (31). As people feel safer and less responsible for what happens, they do things they'd do if they *weren't* driving—talking on the phone, watching videos, reaching for the nearby cup-holder. As Gladwell notes, "That feeling of safety isn't the solution; it's the problem" (32).

Explanation

This passage illustrates a number of things. In the first quoted line, an ellipsis replaces the word "then," a transition in Gladwell's essay that doesn't function well in the new context. The deleted word is within a single quoted sentence, so there's no added period—only the three required for an ellipsis.

This ellipsis is not placed in square brackets because Gladwell's original passage contains no ellipsis of his own. Replacing Gladwell's "we" with the bracketed "American drivers" keeps the point of view consistent with the third person used in the rest of the paragraph. The brackets acknowledge the change. Because the same page of Gladwell's essay is used again twice in the same paragraph, the page number is not presented until the final use of the material. It will be clear that the quotations are from the same page. Note that the page number is not part of the quotation but it is part of the sentence, so it is placed after the quotation marks but before the period. In general, select what is relevant and important enough to quote; use the ellipsis to indicate that you have left out material within the original; place the ellipsis within square brackets only if the original passage itself uses spaced periods; use square brackets to designate material added to the original; introduce quoted sources explicitly in your text; make certain that all words (quoted and unquoted) fit together in grammatically complete ways; and provide page numbers (of print sources) after the quotation marks but before the final punctuation of the sentence.

With the proper symbols, you can add, replace, or delete words within quoted material and enjoy considerable flexibility in the way you use quotations. In general, try to keep your use of quotations as straightforward and uncomplicated as you can. Your reader should always be able to tell what has been taken verbatim from a source and what you have done to change the material. Next are a few more suggestions for punctuating quotations within your work.

HOW SHOULD YOU PUNCTUATE QUOTATIONS?

INTRODUCING A QUOTATION

If you are introducing a quotation with a grammatically complete statement (an independent clause), follow the opening with a colon:

> According to Naomi Klein, the increase in the power of corporations can be traced back to a single, seemingly harmless idea that was popular in the mid-1980s: "that successful corporations must primarily produce brands, as opposed to products" (3).

In this example, the part of the sentence that precedes the colon is grammatically complete. It could end where the colon is without resulting in a sentence fragment. A colon is the proper punctuation mark only if what precedes the colon is grammatically complete. What follows the colon may be a word, a phrase, a sentence, or even a paragraph.

Use a comma if what you are quoting is a complete sentence but your introduction to it makes the quotation itself the necessary object of a verb:

> He said, "I never met her before that occasion."

In this sentence, the verb "said" requires an object (in this case the quotation itself). "He said" is grammatically incomplete, so it is followed by a comma, not a colon. Rephrased as a complete sentence, the introductory phrase requires a colon:

> His denial was emphatic: "I never met her before that occasion."

In the above sentence, if a comma followed the word "emphatic," the result would be a comma splice, because two grammatically independent clauses would be joined without a conjunction.

When you quote single words or phrases from an author, your punctuation should be exactly the same as if the quotation marks were not there. Don't insert unnecessary commas. As I did above, when I wrote that Nick called Gatsby's guests "moths," you should simply use the quoted word without any preceding comma.

ENDING A QUOTATION

At the end of a quoted passage, you should provide whatever end punctuation serves your grammatical needs. If you stop quoting from a passage that ends with a punctuation mark, you may drop the original punctuation mark and provide whatever is grammatically appropriate within your text. In American usage, commas and periods are always placed *inside* the final set of quotation marks, unless you provide a page number in parentheses after the quotation. Note the difference in the two following examples:

> Throughout *America's Meltdown*, John Arden calls American culture the lowest common denominator or "LCD society."

> John Arden calls American culture the lowest common denominator or "LCD society" (1).

The page number in parentheses is not part of the quotation, so it is placed outside the quotation marks, but it is part of the sentence, so it precedes the final period. Semicolons, colons, question marks, and exclamation points always appear *outside* the final quotation marks (unless the question mark or exclamation is part of the quotation).

PRESENTING QUOTATIONS WITHIN QUOTATIONS

When you quote a passage that itself uses quotation marks, change the author's original double quotation marks to single ones to indicate a quotation within a quotation:

Original (from page 7 of Rachel Carson's *The Silent Spring*):
Since the mid-1940s over 200 basic chemicals have been created for use in killing insects, weeds, rodents, and other organisms described in the modern vernacular as "pests"; and they are sold under several thousand different brand names.

Your use of the material:
According to Rachel Carson, more than 200 chemicals are used to kill "organisms described in the modern vernacular as 'pests'" (7).

Notice that the original double quotation marks are changed to single ones to distinguish them from the ones you've provided. Because the quoted passage is presented in the text, instead of set off in block format, the page number is placed outside the quotation marks but before the period. If no page number were provided, the final period would be placed inside *both* sets of closing quotation marks.

PUNCTUATING TITLES

Whenever you provide the title of a work, you should punctuate it properly. Titles of long works, originally published independently, should be underlined (or italicized). Titles of novels, magazines, plays, books, television shows, films, and speeches are all underlined. Titles of essays, short poems, short songs, articles, episodes from a television series, and short stories are all placed in quotation marks. If you quote a published review that punctuates titles differently, you may change the way the title is presented in what you quote without indicating that you have done so. Most magazines, for example, put titles of films in quotation marks. If you quote such a review, you should underline the title or italicize it to attain stylistic consistency in what you've written.

QUOTING POETRY

One final situation needs explanation here: quoting lines of poetry. One important difference between poetry and prose is that lines of poetry are usually shorter than the full printed width of the paper. The line breaks are an important feature of the poem's form. Thus, if you are quoting a section of a poem that, in the original, runs onto another line, you should indicate where the line ends by providing a spaced slash mark where the break occurs. For example, the opening sentence in Adrienne Rich's "Diving into the Wreck" reads (lines 1–7),

> First having read the book of myths,
> and loaded the camera,
> and checked the edge of the knife-blade,
> I put on
> the body-armor of black rubber
> the absurd flippers
> the grave and awkward mask.

If you wish to quote the entire sentence, present it in block format, as I did above, preserving all of the original spacing and line breaks (without slash marks). If you wish to quote fewer than three lines, present them as part of your regular paragraph (not in block format), but provide slash marks to show where her original lines were broken, as in the following example:

> In her poem "Diving into the Wreck," Adrienne Rich assumes that our history of the past is a largely fictionalized "book of myths," a metaphoric place that is dangerous for the female explorer because historians have traditionally neglected the actions of women in their accounts of our past. To document what really occurred in history, she "loaded the camera" to record the events, she "checked the edge of the knife-blade" that she might need to protect herself or to pry beneath superficial appearances, and she put on "the body-armor of black rubber / the absurd flippers / the grave and awkward mask." To Rich, exploring the past is a dangerous but valuable enterprise that requires much preparation.

This paragraph illustrates much of the same selection and introduction of the quoted material that I discussed earlier. The relevant phrases have all been grammatically worked into the author's own phrasing, so that all the words, quoted and original, produce grammatical and coherent sentences. When the quoted lines break in the original, those breaks have been marked with spaced slash marks. Marking such breaks in this fashion is important only in quoting lines of poetry within your regular text, and failure to do so ignores an important feature of the original poem.

QUOTATION MARKS AND OTHER PUNCTUATION

Below are some more examples that illustrate a variety of punctuation circumstances.

A semicolon following a quotation:
Nick calls Gatsby's guests "moths"; perhaps he is not so impartial after all.

A colon following a quotation:
Emma cited several reasons for what she called her "unrestrained rage": Cathy's arrogance, Tom's indifference, and Jackie's boredom.

A quotation with an exclamation point and parenthetical page number:
The technician said, "That lapse in procedure is inexcusable!" (16).

A quotation with an exclamation point followed by attribution:
"That lapse in procedure is inexcusable!" said the technician (16).

A quoted question:
The task force sought to answer one question: "Why did the bridge collapse?"

A quoted question and parenthetical page number:
In *The Culture of Fear*, Barry Glassner asks, "Why, as crime rates plunged throughout the 1990s, did two-thirds of Americans believe they were soaring?" (xi).

A quoted phrase that is part of a question you ask:
At what point did the corporation become entirely self-serving and no longer a "public institution whose purpose was to serve national interests and advance the public good" (Bakan 153)?

HOW SHOULD YOU SELECT AND CITE ELECTRONIC AND INTERNET SOURCES?

The Internet and the proliferation of other electronic and online resources have made information more readily available than ever before. But the variety of such materials has also greatly increased the need for you to critically assess the information you find. The ease with which you can move from site to site, click on links, shrink and open new windows, and cut and paste information to notepads or to documents—this rapid movement from source to source practically *encourages* sloppy and unethical uses of copyrighted information and wording. The format of the Web creates the dangerous illusion that the items you find on it are free and/or public property, akin to common knowledge that isn't owned by an author. Unlike printed material in a library, the information on an electronic source is subject to frequent change, and if you haven't been careful to copy all of the information you will need at the time you see it (or better yet, printed a hard copy of the page), you might lose your access to it, if the text has been revised. A Web page might not even list an author's name, and a particular page to which you might have been linked might not present any publishing information or context for the material on your screen.

Browsing the Web seems like—and often *is*—a form of leisurely entertainment, and your habits during recreation can have dire consequences if they spill over into your writing and suspend the careful sorts of critical thinking and responsible note-taking that are essential to responsible professional and academic writing. Further, the visual similarities among different kinds of documents, when all are filtered through a browser or computer, tend to blur distinctions among them, to make them all seem equal in their reliability or authority. But there are extreme differences among the kinds of material you can view online. Despite all of these challenges, you can learn to sort the nonsense and idiocy from the truly relevant and reputable, and you can use the information with the same scrutiny and care that persuasive writers learn to apply to all that they read.

Much of the early praise for the potential of the Internet focused on the freedom of access to it as a means of publishing—as if the Internet represented the full realization of a democracy in which all people could publish and read virtually everything. At a local level, that freedom takes the form of policies of many Internet service providers that grant all subscribers some space on the server to launch their own websites. In effect, anyone who subscribes to an Internet service may post information.

One practical effect of this accessibility is that the millions of documents and images available from a terminal represent a complete mix of wholly valuable and reputable information with information that is biased, deceptive, or totally unimportant. With careful attention to the source, meticulous critical assessment of evidence and authority, and some detective work, you may find highly useful and credible information related to your topic. For example, major newspapers, magazines, and news organizations usually have websites—often electronic editions of or supplements to their publications and broadcasts. When you know the agency or organization that hosts the site, and the site has been assembled with the same care and editorial standards as the organization's other work, you may rely on the website with as much confidence as you would the print publication or broadcast.

Intermixed with online journals are countless commercial sites, individuals' Web pages and blogs, university sites, government sites, nonprofit agency pages, and highly varied other electronic forums for exchange of information. A U.S. government electronic archive of Senate hearings might be a click or two away from a child's hobby page. Readings posted on the Web by a professor might seem to blend seamlessly with essays written by her students. Always consider the source. The nature of your topic will assist you in determining if a particular site is relevant to your project.

SOURCE RELIABILITY: A SAMPLE TOPIC

An example will illustrate a few of the challenges involved in assessing the reliability of websites. Suppose you are writing an essay on the proposal to permit exploratory drilling for oil in Alaska's Arctic National Wildlife Refuge (ANWR). Entering "ANWR oil exploration" in any of the large Internet search engines (*Yahoo*, for example) will yield links to many related sites. The sheer variety of them should suggest that you need to choose a highly precise focus to make the topic manageable in an essay. That proposal involves issues of natural resource preservation, the international oil market, national security, electoral politics, ecological effects (themselves a highly varied lot), effects on other regional industries (like salmon), anthropological concerns, and a host of other issues. If your topic is any one of these, you will need to sift through contentious and contradictory claims by the involved parties: the oil corporations, the political figures (national and state), interest groups (on many sides), scientists, economists, lawyers, indigenous peoples, labor unions, and environmentalists. Many of these sources will simply be too biased by self-interest to serve as reputable authorities. But if your essay focuses on the conduct of the arguments themselves, on the *rhetoric* of some focused aspect of the debate, then virtually any of these sources could become primary material. The language and argument employed by various parties could become your topic as they illustrate various techniques of argument and propaganda.

A fifteen-minute search of the topic reveals that the national interest in this proposal has energized public relations efforts on the part of industry and environmental groups—to name just two general sides in the debate. The sophistication of such efforts complicates one's attempts to find balanced discussions of the topic—at least on Internet sites. The well-funded participants in this debate have learned the advantages of paying for prominence in the search engine results. Many of the links that appear among the first ten on Google or Yahoo have not been selected by an impartial search program according to their relevance. Google and Yahoo are commercial sites that sell those positions. You will need to search with varied keywords and scroll through many pages of results to find different perspectives. There is certainly no correlation between a site's placement in the search results and its reliability as an authority for research purposes.

You should pay attention to the URL domain of the sites you find—the kind of abbreviation that follows the dot, whether "com," "net," "org," "edu," or "gov." The advocacy groups—whether for the oil industry or for environmental concerns—realize that readers are rightly suspicious of sites with a ".com" domain, as this signifies the for-profit purpose of the site. So they've formed organizations or connections with universities that permit them to use ".org" and ".edu" domains. On a politically charged topic like oil exploration in Alaska, it might also be the case that U.S. government sites (with "gov" domains) are urging particular policies or legislative initiatives. The management of public information is, of course, a strategic effort—one that may or may not yield reliable information with a basis in fact. Little is as it appears to be in the cyberspace battle for public opinion. Remaining skeptical, seeking evidence of bias or agenda, and being persistent in identifying the members and missions of organizations will be crucial whenever you're looking at Web resources on complicated, hot national topics.

Most of the websites discussing Alaskan oil exploration foreground their credibility in sometimes transparent ways. For example, one site, called simply "anwr.org," describes its parent organization, Arctic Power, as a "grassroots, non-profit citizen's organization with 10,000 members founded in April of 1992 . . ." ("Arctic Power"). The organization emphasizes how comprehensive its membership is:

> Arctic Power membership spans the economic spectrum—including miners, fishermen, loggers, tourism operators, transportation businesses, labor unions, banks, teachers, the legal community, retail firms, service industries, non-profit organizations, Alaska Native corporations, local elected officials, and many others. ("Arctic Power")

The prominent links on its home page certainly make it seem as if it's got this complicated issue covered, attending to veterans, labor, Alaskans, and even caribou. But all of these topics are discussed with one mission in mind: "to expedite congressional and presidential approval of oil exploration and production within the Coastal Plain of the Arctic National Wildlife Refuge" ("Arctic Power"). The board of directors for Arctic Power includes representatives of the Alaska Support Industry Alliance, the Alaska State Chamber of Commerce, the Resource Development Council, the Alaska Miner's Association, and the Alaska Oil & Gas Association. On the one hand, having such members on its board gives the group insight into corporate positions on the issue. On the other, it casts doubt on the extent to which the group is truly a "grassroots" movement, representing a citizen's initiative. Its site offers brief arguments, sometimes called "talking points," in quick tours of the topic. And it asks readers to use its "Action Center" to e-mail Congressional representatives, to petition Congress, and to blog in support of oil drilling. The rhetoric of the site is a mix of seeming neutrality and energetically partisan advocacy. Like other oil-industry funded groups with "org" domains, this one works to gain credibility as a moderate group with broad support, and then engages in passionate and one-sided argument.

Similar strategies are employed by groups opposing Alaska drilling, as well. One such group, the Alaska Coalition, describes itself as a "coalition of nearly 1,000 conservation, sporting, labor, and religious groups working together to protect Alaska's wild public land" ("Who We Are"). Claiming to be born of cooperation among nearly a thousand organizations with highly varied missions, the Alaska Coalition offers an organizational self-portrait drawn with many of the same strokes as those used by Arctic Power: cooperation, diversity, populism. And like the site of Arctic Power, the Alaska Coalition's site offers talking points, links to other activist groups, and calls for action and public support—but for conservation not drilling. There are sites more oriented toward information than bandwagon activism, such as one maintained by Ecotrust calling itself "Inforain," a "bioregional information system" ("About Inforain"). Though this site is better documented, calmer, and far more substantive than the Alaska Coalition's site, it is very much a proconservation site and therefore a partisan in the debate.

When you choose a topic fraught with controversy, you need to seek varied points of view and pay meticulous attention to the sorts of evidence provided by the sources and the overall validity of the reasoning they employ. Check the credentials of the principal authors, and attempt to verify the information they provide by consulting additional sources, ideally universities, major news organizations, print publications (ones without economic ties to the interested parties), government documents, and court reports. As this sample topic illustrates, you should be cautious and skeptical of all claims—doubly so when the source is online. The Web has evolved into an enterprise that is chiefly commercial. You should not limit your research to Internet sites, unless such texts are well suited to your topic.

CITING INTERNET WEBSITES

Citing paraphrased or quoted information from Internet sources requires some adaptation of your usual procedures. If you know the name of the author or of the organization, name it in your text as you introduce the material, mentioning the publication medium as you do so (website, CD-ROM, online journal, and so forth). If you are using a particular page from a website, place the title of the page in quotation marks in parentheses at the end of the sentence. Titles of pages or sections within sites are often quite long, and quoting them in your text in their entirety would be cumbersome. In such cases, you need to preserve the first word of the section name (to enable your readers to easily identify it among your list of works cited) and then use an abbreviated or shortened form that refers to the full citation in your list. Writing an abbreviated title isn't always a simple matter. For example, an underlined link on the Natural Resources Defense Council "Wilderness Preservation" page is entitled "In Big Oil's Crosshairs." The page itself, if you click on that link, is headed "The Bush Administration's Unbalanced Plan to Drill in the Western Arctic." In this case, the best thing might be simply to use "Bush Administration's Unbalanced Plan," making certain that the actual full citation is clear in your list of works cited. The format for listing Web pages and sites will differ according to the appropriate style manual for your discipline. And, because the kinds of sources continue to evolve, most of the style manuals offer only provisional guidance and admit that the guidelines will be changing as the media evolve. But all the formats require that your final list include the author or organization (if known), the title of the page, the complete URL (Universal Resource Locator), the latest date that the page was updated (if known), and the date you actually consulted it.

The convenience of consulting websites has two costs: the need to be particularly alert to various ways the sites might be unreliable, and the challenges of citing sometimes tricky documents. It's not always easy to tell who the author is, and you might not find a date that the document was last revised—though you should explore other links on the home page to try to find this information. You may not know whether a title should be presented as a part of a whole (and placed in quotation marks) or as a site on its own (and underlined or italicized). Remember to consult the latest edition of the style manual for the discipline in which you are writing, and make certain that you do two things:

1. Provide the complete URL, with totally accurate transcription of every symbol (including slash marks and underlines) as it appears in the location box of your browser. If it is so long that you must break the line, do so only *after* one of the slash marks. The Modern Language Association asks that you enclose the URL in angle brackets, < >, to clearly signify its status.
2. Make certain that you provide the date that you consulted the site. Below are citations as they would appear in a list of works cited in MLA format:

A reference to a website:

Arctic Monitoring and Assessment Programme (AMAP) Homepage. AMAP. 2 August 2006. <http://www.amap.no>.

A reference to one page from a website:

"Asthma and Air Pollution." 8 June 2005. Natural Resources Defense Council. 2 August 2006. <http://www.nrdc.org/health/effects/fasthma.asp>.

OTHER ELECTRONIC SOURCES

Your computer might be linked to some databases to which your university or employer subscribes. Because you gain access to these databases with your Internet browser, they might seem like ordinary websites, but they are actually distinct from the Internet. One such database is *LexisNexis Academic*, frequently available on campuses. LexisNexis offers searchable, computerized archives of published documents. This powerful—and expensive—service is a highly useful means of gaining access to electronic versions of materials originally published in a variety of media: newspapers, magazines, journals, newsletters, trade publications, and abstracts. LexisNexis enables you to view and print information directly from your computer without the need to find the printed source in a library. It provides the actual written texts from the original sources but without the graphics, visual layout, and pagination of the originals. Generally believed to be reputably edited and reliable texts, the items found on *LexisNexis Academic* are really distinct versions of the original works. The service does provide the full publication information for the items, but it reformats the document in ways that do not enable you to tell on which page in the document a given sentence or paragraph appears. Because the item has been significantly reformatted from its original form, you must cite the version you consulted, indicating that the material was obtained through LexisNexis. Presumably, the actual words have been transcribed accurately by the editors, but the authority for the accuracy of that transcription now resides at LexisNexis. Your citation should indicate that the online service owns the version you consulted and that what you cite is at one stage of remove from the original printed text.

When consulting such an archive, you need to make yourself familiar with how it works—both with how the search engine enables you to make choices among dates and kinds of materials and with how the service organizes and labels the parts of the original citation. The author's name might be called the "byline"; the title of an article might be called the "headline." The services offer guidance and tips that enable you to figure out how the original citation would be reconstructed from what they provide, and most include a link to some sample citations following various formats. When you cite in your regular text a source obtained through one of these services, use the author's name (if available) or the title, as you would if you were citing the original version. This reference, whether explicit or parenthetical, should clearly identify to which item in your list of works cited the name refers. Unless the service provides the original page numbers, you do not provide them. In your list of works cited, begin by citing the work as you would the original, and then follow it by noting the name of the online service, the name of the institution that subscribed to that service and its location, the date you found the source on the site, and the URL for the site in angle brackets. Consult the appropriate style sheet for your discipline for the exact way of listing such a source. If you've found an item on a service such as *LexisNexis Academic* and have not consulted the original version, you must not cite it without acknowledging the online source.

Other subscription databases that are frequently available at libraries include *InfoTrac* (by Thomson Learning), *Academic Search Premier* and *Business Source Complete* (by EBSCOhost), and *ProQuest*. Like *LexisNexis*, they present the full texts of documents but reformat them in ways that do not preserve the original layout and pagination. Because the original page number for a passage will not be identified by these databases, parenthetical citations to such sources usually will consist of only the author's name. The entry in the list of works cited must acknowledge that the version of the document you consulted was provided by the database. The URL for the actual document is probably long and complicated, often a series of symbols and letters that is a temporary designation. For this reason, you provide the URL for the database, not the one for the document itself.

If the database provides scanned images of the original pages of the publication, as is sometimes done with articles from scholarly journals, then you should provide the page number in your parenthetical citation as you normally would. In your works cited, you still must cite the online archive or service that provided the scanned image. *JSTOR* (Journal Storage) is one such archive. Operated by a nonprofit organization, the *JSTOR* collection spans nearly every discipline and is continually expanding. It does not include current issues of scholarly publications. There is likely to be a gap of several years between the most recent issue and those included in the archive. The *JSTOR* archive greatly expands the availability of scholarly journals and the ease with which they may be consulted. It is crucial that you acknowledge the archive as you cite sources obtained with it—not only to be academically honest but also to support the service.

Below are some citations of documents from subscription databases in MLA format.

Barash, Jeffrey Andrew. "The Sources of Memory." *Journal of the History of Ideas* 58 (1997): 707–17. *JSTOR*. 2 August 2006 <http://www.jstor.org/search>.

"Consumers Consider the Importance of Corporate Social Responsibility." *Strategic Finance*, August 2006: 20–22. *Business Source Complete*. EBSCOhost. Denison University, Granville, OH. 6 August 2006 <http://search.ebscohost.com>.

Dunn, Joseph. "How Electric Cars Came Back from the Dead." *Sunday Times (London)* 23 July 2006: 6. *LexisNexis Academic*. LexisNexis. Denison University, Granville, OH. 6 August 2006 <http://web.lexis-nexis.com/universe>.

Livingstone, Sonia and Ellen J. Helsper. "Does Advertising Literacy Mediate the Effects of Advertising on Children? A Critical Examination of Two Linked Research Literatures in Relation to Obesity and Food Choice." *Journal of Communication* 56 (2006): 560–84. *Academic Search Premier*. EBSCOhost. Denison University, Granville, OH. 6 August 2006 <http://search.epnet.com>.

Don't despair if at first all of these rules seem complicated. Much of this material is probably review, and all of it will become second nature to you with practice. The procedures for quoting and paraphrasing are vitally important, even if they strike you at first as merely cosmetic or surface details. Following these conventions will reassure your readers that you are ethical, competent, and careful. And if all of the papers you write are put in proper form before you turn them in, you free your professor to comment on the substance of what you say—things that probably both of you find more interesting. After all, your professor has only a limited amount of space and time to devote to commenting on your writing, and if your paper is in poor form, you waste valuable time that could be spent on more interesting matters.

Keep this book and refer to it whenever your memory of these conventions fades. On page 52, I've provided a brief checklist. You should consult it while revising papers that employ quoted or paraphrased material.

A FURTHER NOTE ABOUT STYLE MANUALS

Unless you have already chosen a major or a field of specialization, it doesn't make sense for you to purchase the standard style manual for every course you take in different fields. Most writing handbooks include enough information about the major style manuals to suffice in introductory classes. Once you are committed to a field of study, however, it is important for you to purchase the manual that your professor or advisor recommends for that field. You will discover that many of the features of manuscript form, some of the features of writing style, and the formats both for in-text citations and for lists of references at the end of a work differ from one field to the next in significant ways. Learning to apply the guidelines for your field is part of learning the field. It might seem that the differences from one field to the next are tiny, and they might seem arbitrary or merely a matter of a teacher's preference. But the guidelines are not, in fact, arbitrary. They reflect the values and methods of inquiry characteristic of the field to which they apply. For example, when formats in the social sciences seem to emphasize the year of publication, it makes sense because the recentness of information in the natural sciences typically matters more than it might in the humanities. If the social sciences are meticulous about citing all the authors of a multiauthor work, it makes sense because so many research projects involve collaborative or team efforts. You might not always know the reasons for features of the prescribed formats, but your work will appear more mature and professional if you care about and apply the guidelines in the appropriate style manual.

Below are some sample citations, included here only to illustrate a few of the differences among some prominent styles.

An article in a weekly magazine

MLA (*MLA Handbook for Writers of Research Papers*)

Strouse, Jean. "The Unknown J. P. Morgan." The New Yorker 29 March 1999: 66–79.

CMS (*Chicago Manual of Style*)

Strouse, Jean. "The Unknown J. P. Morgan." *The New Yorker*, March 29, 1999, 66–79.

CSE (*Scientific Style and Format*)

Strouse J. 1999 March 29. The unknown J. P. Morgan. New Yorker: 66–79.

APA (*Publication Manual of the American Psychological Association*)

Strouse, J. (1999, March 29). The Unknown J. P. Morgan. *The New Yorker*, 66–79.

APSA (*Style Manual for Political Science*)

Strouse, Jean. 1999. "The Unknown J. P. Morgan." *The New Yorker*, March 29: 66–79.

A book

MLA

Glassner, Barry. The Culture of Fear: Why Americans Are Afraid of the Wrong Things. New York: Basic Books, 1999.

CMS

Glassner, Barry. *The Culture of Fear: Why Americans Are Afraid of the Wrong Things*. New York: Basic Books, 1999.

CSE

Glassner B. 1999. The culture of fear: why Americans are afraid of the wrong things. New York: Basic Books. 276 p.

APA

Glassner, B. (1999). *The Culture of Fear: Why Americans Are Afraid of the Wrong Things*. New York: Basic Books.

APSA

Glassner, Barry. 1999. *The Culture of Fear: Why Americans Are Afraid of the Wrong Things*. New York: Basic Books.

A website

MLA

Sierra Club. Home page. 2006. Sierra Club. 2 August 2006 <http://www.sierraclub.org/>.

CMS

Sierra Club. Sierra Club home page. 2006. http://www.sierraclub.org/ (August 2, 2006).

CSE

Sierra Club. 2006. Sierra Club home page. <http://www.sierraclub.org/>. Accessed 2006 Aug. 2.

APA

Sierra Club. (2006). Sierra Club home page. Retrieved August 2, 2006, from http://www.sierraclub.org/.

APSA

Sierra Club. 2006. Sierra Club Home Page. http://www.sierraclub.org/ (accessed Aug. 2, 2006).

REVISION CHECKLIST FOR QUOTING AND PARAPHRASING

1. Are all of your paragraphs developed adequately, with evidence for your argument or illustration of your complex ideas? Is the paragraph primarily your words, with quotations or paraphrased evidence serving only as supporting material? Do you provide too much information from sources, or too little?
2. If you have paraphrased, did you introduce the material from your source to indicate clearly what is from the source? Did you mention the author? Did you provide a note or a parenthetical citation of the source so that your readers would have all the information they need to locate the source and page from which the information comes?
3. Is the wording of paraphrased material entirely your own? Does it accurately reflect the viewpoint expressed in the original?
4. If you quote, have you introduced each passage, or does your context make it clear that the words are quoted from a source? Have you followed the quotation with a page number or with a note? Is each quoted passage introduced sufficiently so that quoted words fit together grammatically with your own, to assure that your reader will understand the significance of the passage?
5. Are quoted words in proper form? Are they quoted accurately and marked by quotation marks? Have any added words or letters been placed in square brackets, and have deleted words been replaced by an

ellipsis? Have you indicated the line breaks in quoted poetry with slash marks? Have you punctuated the quotations properly?

6. Have you followed all quotations, particularly longer, block quotations, with your own analysis or interpretation of the passages? Are the transitions to and from quoted material smooth and coherent?
7. In your citations of websites, have you made certain that the URL is typed correctly and provided the date that you consulted the source?
8. If you've consulted sources that have been indexed and re-presented by an online database, have you noted the online version that you have cited?
9. Have you followed the format for citations required by the style manual that is used in your discipline? Do all of your citations present all of the necessary information about the works you consulted?

APPENDIX: INTERNET RESOURCES

This section presents useful websites organized by disciplines within the humanities and social sciences. Some of these sites provide resources for research within a discipline, and some provide guides for writing papers and citing sources. Each discipline has its own resources and its own rules, so these sites provide an introduction to these resources and rules. They barely scratch the surface of what's available on the Internet, but they should provide a good start.

ANTHROPOLOGY

American Anthropological Association Resources on the Internet
AAA's list of links of interest to anthropologists.
http://www.aaanet.org/resinet.htm

Anthropology in the News
Contains the latest findings throughout anthropology. Maintained by Texas A&M University.
http://www.tamu.edu/anthropology/news.html

Society of American Archaeology Links
This site has a list of references for archaeologists and archaeology students.
http://saa.org/links.html

Voice of the Shuttle: Anthropology and Archaeology Pages
These sites have references to a wide range of current writings from anthropologists and archaeologists, as well as general resources.
http://vos.ucsb.edu

WWW Virtual Library: Anthropology
General anthropology resource with links for each subdiscipline within anthropology.
http://vlib.anthrotech.com

COMMUNICATION

EraM—Ethnicity, Racism, and Media Discussion Forum
This site explores the issues surrounding ethnicity, racism, and the media.
http://www.blackagenda.com/cybercolonies/eram/index.htm

Handouts and Links: Communications
Describes steps for planning and writing papers in communications studies courses, with links to other writing resources, at the Writing Center, University of North Carolina, Chapel Hill.
http://www.unc.edu/depts/wcweb/handouts/communications.html

National Speakers Association
Resources for speakers, whether professional or amateur.
http://www.nsaspeaker.org

Online Communication Studies Resources
This site contains an index of online resources for communication studies, including advertising, film studies, and political communication. Maintained by the Department of Communication Studies at the University of Iowa.
http://www.uiowa.edu/~commstud/resources

Political Communication Resources
A gateway to Internet sites containing useful information about the media and democracy.
http://depts.washington.edu/bennett/

Toastmasters International
Tips for making speeches put together by Toastmasters International.
http://www.toastmasters.org/pdfs/top10.pdf

Voice of the Shuttle: Media Studies Page

This site has references to a wide range of current writings from media studies scholars, as well as general resources.
http://vos.ucsb.edu

ENGLISH AND COMPOSITION

Elements of Style

The online version of the popular English composition handbook.
http://www.bartleby.com/141

EServer Rhetoric and Composition

Links to resources in rhetoric and composition.
http://www.rhetoric.eserver.org

Literature and Composition Resources

Maintained by Frostburg State University, a guide to quality resources, both primary and secondary, on the Web.
http://faculty.frostburg.edu/engl/gartner/Litcomp.htm

Modern Language Association

Official website of the MLA. Includes a section on frequently asked questions about MLA style as well as links to resources and publications.
http://www.mla.org

The OWL at Purdue

An online writing lab offering free writing help and teaching resources. Maintained by Purdue University.
http://owl.english.purdue.edu

Resources for Writers and Writing Instructors

Links to a number of writing resources, maintained by Jack Lynch at Rutgers University.
http://andromeda.rutgers.edu/~jlynch/Writing/links.html

Writing@CSU

"Home of Colorado State University's online learning environment, the Writing Studio. Use this site to learn to write, save your work in a private password-protected account, and get feedback on your writing."
http://writing.colostate.edu

FILM STUDIES

American Film Institute
AFI is a national institute providing leadership in screen education.
http://www.afi.com

Dartmouth Writing Program
Features tips for writing about film.
http://www.dartmouth.edu/~writing/materials/student/humanities/film.shtml

George Mason University Writing Center Guide to Writing about Film
This useful guide for film writing includes questions to consider when writing about film and cinematic elements to "read." Contains useful resources.
http://www.gmu.edu/departments/writingcenter/handouts/film.html

IFILM
A film portal and directory with editorial information and links to over 5,000 domestic and foreign Internet films.
http://www.ifilm.com

The Internet Movie Database
An award-winning movie website that includes reviews of current movies, message boards, and a vast database of films.
http://www.imdb.com

Movie Review Query Engine
A guide to film reviews.
http://www.mrqe.com

Sandhills Community College
Guidelines for writing about film.
http://www.sandhills.cc.nc.us/english/shared/160guidelines.html

GEOGRAPHY

About Geography
A list of current articles on geography in the news, as well as general resources.
http://geography.about.com

Internet Resources for Geographers

General resources for geography. Maintained by the Department of Geography at the University of Colorado, Boulder.
http://www.colorado.edu/geography/virtdept/resources/contents.htm

Internet Resources for Geography and Geology

General resources for geography and geology. Maintained by the University of Wisconsin, Stevens Point.
http://www.uwsp.edu/geo/internet/geog_geol_resources.html

Map Projections Poster

Map projections resources maintained by the U.S. Geological Survey.
http://mac.usgs.gov/mac/isb/pubs/MapProjections/projections.html

Maps and Cartography

Earth Science and Map Library Map Collection at the University of California, Berkeley.
http://www.lib.berkeley.edu/EART/MapCollections.html

New Books in Geography

A list of new books in geography. Maintained by the Association of American Geographers.
http://www.aag.org/nbig/index.cfm

HISTORY

Dartmouth Writing Program

A student guide to writing a history paper, provided by Dartmouth College.
http://www.dartmouth.edu/~writing/materials/student/soc_sciences/history.shtml

History

General resources for history organized by historical time period.
http://www.scholiast.org/history

History Matters

History Matters serves as a gateway to Web resources and offers other useful materials for teaching U.S. history.
http://historymatters.gmu.edu

History Writing Guides
Guide to reading and interpreting primary sources. Very helpful for researchers.
http://academic.bowdoin.edu/WritingGuides

History and Theory
This website and online journal is devoted to exploring the links between philosophy and history.
http://www.historyandtheory.org

Voice of the Shuttle: History Page
This site has references to a wide range of writings from world historians, as well as general resources.
http://vos.ucsb.edu

Women's Biographies: Distinguished Women of Past and Present
This site is devoted to the history of women throughout the world.
http://www.DistinguishedWomen.com

World History Matters
World History Matters is a portal to world history links on the Web.
http://worldhistorymatters.org

WWW VL The World Wide Web Virtual Library: History Index
General resource with links to many history resources. Maintained by the University of Kansas.
http://vlib.iue.it/history

JOURNALISM

The Associated Press Style Book
An important style guide for all popular publications. People who do public relations and advertising generally follow AP style as well in their writing. It is also a good guide for general writing.
http://www.apstylebook.com

Association for Education in Journalism and Mass Communication Links
A list of links to appropriate, noncommercial websites of interest to members of the Association for Education in Journalism and Mass Communication.
http://www.aejmc.org/links

JournalismNet

JournalismNet is an extensive list of resources for journalists, including daily news updates.

http://www.journalismnet.com

The Journalist's Toolbox

The Journalist's Toolbox contains links to areas of interest to journalists, as well as teaching tools for editors and professors. Maintained by the American Press Institute.

http://www.americanpressinstitute.org/pages/toolbox

The Poynter Center

A resource for writing about news and current affairs.

http://poynter.org

Project for Excellence in Journalism: Understanding News in the Information Age

The website of the Project for Excellence in Journalism, a research organization that specializes in using empirical methods to evaluate and study the performance of the press. Features news and links to other resources.

http://www.journalism.org

Robert Niles Journalism Help

Basic statistics for journalists or other laypersons.

http://www.robertniles.com

Society of Professional Journalists

The website of the Society of Professional Journalists, a large and broad-based, national journalism organization.

http://www.spj.org

PHILOSOPHY

The American Philosophical Association's Web Resources

A list of philosophical associations and societies, centers and institutes, and electronic texts. Maintained by the American Philosophical Association.

http://www.apa.udel.edu/apa/resources

Dartmouth Writing Program
A student guide to writing a philosophy paper, provided by Dartmouth College.
http://www.dartmouth.edu/~writing/materials/student/humanities/philosophy.shtml

Descartes' Meditations Home Page
This site contains an online edition of Descartes' classic work of philosophical reflections.
http://www.wright.edu/cola/descartes

Ethics Updates Home Page
This site contains resources on the following topics: moral theory, relativism, pluralism, religion, and egoism.
http://ethics.acusd.edu/

Philosophers: Main Page
This site provides easy access to resources in philosophy, categorized by philosopher.
http://www.epistemelinks.com/Main/MainPers.asp

Philosophy Comix
This site contains examples of philosophical topics from contemporary comic strips.
http://members.aol.com/lshauser/phlcomix.html

Philosophy News Service
A list of contemporary news in philosophy.
http://www.philosophynews.com/PNS

Philosophy Pages
This site focuses on Web links to Western philosophy sites.
http://www.philosophypages.com/index.htm

Philosophy, Introduction
This site provides a general overview of what philosophy is.
http://pespmc1.vub.ac.be/PHILOSI.html

Stanford Encyclopedia of Philosophy
An extensive online encyclopedia of philosophy.
http://plato.stanford.edu

Voice of the Shuttle: Philosophy Page

This site has references to a wide range of writings from philosophers, as well as general resources.
http://vos.ucsb.edu

POLITICAL SCIENCE

Inter-university Consortium for Political and Social Research Front Page

This site contains social science data and resources for researchers.
http://www.icpsr.umich.edu/

Resources for Political Science

A list of political science organizations, research in progress, and upcoming publications. Maintained by the American Political Science Association.
http://apsanet.org/section_188.cfm

Voice of the Shuttle: Politics and Government Page

This site has references to a wide range of writings from scholars of politics and government, as well as general resources.
http://vos.ucsb.edu

WWW Resources for Political Scientists

This site contains links to political science resources organized by topic and type of resource. Maintained by the University of Colorado, Boulder.
http://osiris.colorado.edu/POLSCI/links.html

RELIGION

AAR Other Resources

The American Academy of Religion's list of other resources for religious studies scholars.
http://www.aarweb.org/other/default.asp

Dartmouth Writing Program

A student guide to writing a religion paper, provided by Dartmouth College.
http://www.dartmouth.edu/~writing/materials/student/humanities/religion.shtml

Voice of the Shuttle: Religious Studies Page
This site has references to a wide range of general religious studies resources, as well as links to sites dedicated to the thinkings of many major religious and spiritual groups.
http://vos.ucsb.edu

SOCIOLOGY

American Sociological Association Manuscript Checklist
http://asanet.org/pubs/notice.pdf

Classical Sociological Theory
This site contains online texts of classical social thinkers. Maintained by the University of Chicago.
http://www.spc.uchicago.edu/ssr1/PRELIMS/theory.html

Dartmouth Writing Program
A student guide to writing a sociology paper, provided by Dartmouth College.
http://www.dartmouth.edu/~writing/materials/student/soc_sciences/sociology.shtml

Online Communication Studies Resources
This site contains an index of online resources for cultural studies. Maintained by the Department of Communication Studies at the University of Iowa.
http://www.uiowa.edu/~commstud/resources

Social Science Hub
Excellent starting point for research. Comprehensive enough to include many of the major categories within the discipline.
http://www.sshub.com/

SociologyOnline
This British site for all students of sociology, criminology, and social thought is full of information about both classical and contemporary thinkers.
http://www.sociologyonline.co.uk/

SocioSite

This site, maintained by the University of Amsterdam, provides a global perspective on sociology with access to a number of European theorists.
http://www.sociosite.net/index.php

Voice of the Shuttle: Cultural Studies Page

This site has references to a wide range of current sociological thinkers, many specifically oriented toward cultural theories.
http://vos.ucsb.edu

APPENDIX B

SUGGESTED READINGS FOR *LET NOBODY TURN US AROUND*

SECTION ONE: FOUNDATIONS: SLAVERY AND ABOLITIONISM, 1768–1861

Anne Applegate, "Phillis Wheatley: Her Critics and Her Contribution," *Negro American Literature Forum,* 9, no. 4 (1975), pp. 123–126.

Sterling Allen Brown, "Remembering Nat Turner," *Callaloo,* 21, no. 4 (1998), pp. 725–726.

Vincent Carretta, and Philip Gould, eds., *Genius in Bondage: Literature of the Early Black Atlantic* (Lexington: University Press of Kentucky, 2001).

Henry Louis Gates, Jr., "The Day When America Decided That Blacks Were of a Species That Could Create Literature," *Journal of Blacks in Higher Education,* 5 (1994), pp. 50–51.

Kathy L. Glass, *Courting Communities: Black Female Nationalism and "Syncre-Nationalism" in the Nineteenth-Century North* (New York: Routledge, 2006).

Sharon Harley and Black Women and Work Collective, eds., *Sister Circle: Black Women and Work* (New Brunswick: Rutgers University Press, 2002).

Lucy Hayden, "Classical Tidings for Africa Muse: Phillis Wheatley's Use of Greek and Roman Mythology," *CLA Journal,* 35, no. 4 (1992), pp. 432–447.

Darlene Clark Hine, *Black Women in United States History*. 4 vols. (Brooklyn: Carlson Publishing, 1990).

Angelene Jamison, "Analysis of Selected Poetry of Phillis Wheatley," *Journal of Negro Education,* 43, no. 3 (1974), pp. 408–416.

James S. Peters, *The Spirit of David Walker: The Obscure Hero* (Lanham: University Press of America, 2002).

Robin W. Winks, *The Blacks in Canada: A History* (Montreal: McGill-Queen's University Press, 1971).

SECTION TWO: RECONSTRUCTION AND REACTION: THE AFTERMATH OF SLAVERY AND THE DAWN OF SEGREGATION, 1861-1915

Hakim Adi, and Marika Sherwood, *Pan-African History: Political Figures from Africa and the Diaspora since 1787* (London: Routledge, 2003).

Stephen Ward Angell, and Anthony B. Pinn, *Social Protest Thought in the African Methodist Episcopal Church, 1862–1939* (Knoxville: University of Tennessee Press, 2000).

Jinx C. Broussard, *Giving a Voice to the Voiceless: Four Pioneering Black Women Journalists* (New York: Routledge, 2004).

Stanley Crouch, and Playthell Benjamin, *Reconsidering the Souls of Black Folk* (Philadelphia: Running Press, 2002).

Thomas Dublin, Franchesca Arias, and Debora Carreras, *What Gender Perspectives Shaped the Emergence of the National Association of Colored Women, 1895–1920?* (Binghamton: State University of New York, 2000).

Gene Andrew Jarrett, and Thomas Lewis Morgan, eds., *The Complete Stories of Paul Laurence Dunbar* (Athens: Ohio University Press, 2005).

Cookie Lommel, *Mary Church Terrell: Speaking out for Civil Rights* (Berkeley Heights: Enslow, 2003). (juv. lit)

Emily Oswald, "Imagining Race: Illustrating the Poems of Paul Laurence Dunbar," *Book History*, 9 (2006), pp. 213–233.

SECTION THREE: FROM PLANTATION TO GHETTO: THE GREAT MIGRATION, HARLEM RENAISSANCE, AND WORLD WAR, 1915-1954

David Aretha, *The Trial of the Scottsboro Boys* (Greensboro: Morgan Reynolds Pub., 2007).

Carolyn LaDelle Bennett, ed., *An Annotated Bibliography of Mary Mcleod Bethune's Chicago Defender Columns, 1948–1955* (Lewiston: Edwin Mellen Press, 2001).

Mary McLeod Bethune, and Carolyn LaDelle Bennett, *No Room for Despair: How to Hope in Troubled Times: Mary Mcleod Bethune's Cold War Integration-Era Commentary* (Baltimore: Publish America, 2006).

Robert Blaisdell, ed., *Selected Writings and Speeches of Marcus Garvey* (Mineola: Dover Publications, 2004).

Andrea Broadwater, *Mary Mcleod Bethune: Educator and Activist* (Berkeley Heights: Enslow Publishers, 2003).

Floris Loretta Barnett Cash, *African American Women and Social Action: The Clubwomen and Volunteerism from Jim Crow to the New Deal, 1896–1936* (Westport: Greenwood Press, 2001).

Elizabeth Clark-Lewis, *Living In, Living Out: African American Domestics in Washington, D.C., 1910–1940* (Washington: Smithsonian Institution Press, 1994).

Sara L. Creed, and Hasia Diner, *How Did Women Shape the Discourse and Further Interracial Cooperation in the Worldwide Mass Movement to "Free the Scottsboro Boys"?* (Binghamton: State University of New York, 2003).

Michael D. Davis, and Hunter R. Clark, *Thurgood Marshall: Warrior at the Bar, Rebel on the Bench* (New York: Carol Publishing Group, 1992).

Joseph Dorinson, and William Pencak, eds., *Paul Robeson: Essays on His Life and Legacy* (Jefferson, N.C.: McFarland, 2002).

Nikki Giovanni, *Shimmy Shimmy Shimmy Like My Sister Kate: Looking at the Harlem Renaissance through Poems* (New York: H. Holt, 1996). (juv.)

Earl Ofari Hutchinson, *Blacks and Reds: Race and Class in Conflict, 1919–1990* (East Lansing: Michigan State University Press, 1995).

Lloyd D. McCarthy, *In-Dependence from Bondage: Claude Mckay and Michael Manley: Defying the Ideological Clash and Policy Gaps in African Diaspora Relations* (Trenton: Africa World Press, 2007).

Wilson Jeremiah Moses, ed., *Classical Black Nationalism: From the American Revolution to Marcus Garvey* (New York: New York University Press, 1996).

Venetria K. Patton, and Maureen Honey, eds., *Double-Take: A Revisionist Harlem Renaissance Anthology* (New Brunswick: Rutgers University Press, 2001).

Lemoine D. Pierce, ed., *A Research Guide to the Life and Legislative Achievements of Congressman Adam Clayton Powell, Jr.* (Atlanta: Auburn Avenue Research Library on African-American Culture and History, 1999).

Michelle Ann Stephens, *Black Empire: The Masculine Global Imaginary of Caribbean Intellectuals in the United States, 1914–1962* (Durham: Duke University Press, 2005).

Jeffrey C. Stewart, Center Paul Robeson Cultural, and Museum Jane Voorhees Zimmerli Art, eds., *Paul Robeson: Artist and Citizen* (New Brunswick: Rutgers University Press, 1998).

Clarence Taylor, *Black Religious Intellectuals: The Fight for Equality from Jim Crow to the Twenty-first Century* (New York: Routledge, 2002).

Cynthia Taylor, *A. Philip Randolph: The Religious Journey of an African American Labor Leader* (New York: New York University Press, 2006).

Ula Y. Taylor, "Negro Women Are Great Thinkers as Well as Doers: Amy Jacques-Garvey and Community Feminism, 1924–1927," *Journal of Women's History,* 12, no. 2 (2000), pp. 104–126.

Steven C. Tracy, ed., *A Historical Guide to Langston Hughes* (New York: Oxford University Press, 2004).

Juan Williams, *Thurgood Marshall: American Revolutionary* (New York: Times Books, 1998).

Robert H. Zieger, *For Jobs and Freedom: Race and Labor in America since 1865* (Lexington: University Press of Kentucky, 2007).

SECTION FOUR: WE SHALL OVERCOME: THE SECOND RECONSTRUCTION, 1954–1975

Russell Freedman, *Freedom Walkers: The Story of the Montgomery Bus Boycott* (New York: Holiday House, 2006). (juv.)

Davis W. Houck, and David E. Dixon, eds., *Rhetoric, Religion and the Civil Rights Movement, 1954–1965* (Waco: Baylor University Press, 2006).

J. L. Jeffries, ed., *Comrades: A Local History of the Black Panther Party* (Bloomington: Indiana University Press, 2007).

Charles Richard Johnson, and Bob Adelman, *King: The Photobiography of Martin Luther King, Jr.* (New York: Viking Studio, 2000).

Dorothee E. Kocks, *Dream a Little: Land and Social Justice in Modern America* (Berkeley: University of California Press, 2000).

Peter J. Ling, and Sharon Monteith, eds., *Gender and the Civil Rights Movement* (New Brunswick: Rutgers University Press, 2004).

Elizabeth Sutherland Martínez, ed., *Letters from Mississippi* (New York: McGraw-Hill, 1965).

Calvin Craig Miller, *Roy Wilkins: Leader of the NAACP* (Greensboro: Morgan Reynolds, 2005). (juv.)

Margo V. Perkins, *Autobiography as Activism: Three Black Women of the Sixties* (Jackson: University Press of Mississippi, 2000).

Renee Christine Romano, and Leigh Raiford, eds., *The Civil Rights Movement in American Memory* (Athens: University of Georgia Press, 2006).

Rosetta E. Ross, *Witnessing and Testifying: Black Women, Religion, and Civil Rights* (Minneapolis: Fortress Press, 2003).
Stephen Shames, and Charles E. Jones, *The Black Panthers: Photographs* (New York: Aperture, 2006).
Mary Stanton, *Journey toward Justice: Juliette Hampton Morgan and the Montgomery Bus Boycott* (Athens: University of Georgia Press, 2006).
James A. Tyner, *The Geography of Malcolm X: Black Radicalism and the Remaking of American Space* (New York: Routledge, 2006).
Robert Weisbrot, *Marching toward Freedom, 1957–1965: From the Founding of the Southern Christian Leadership Conference to the Assassination of Malcom X* (New York: Chelsa House, 1994). (juv.)
Sondra K. Wilson, ed., *In Search of Democracy: The NAACP Writings of James Weldon Johnson, Walter White, and Roy Wilkins (1920–1977)* (New York: Oxford University Press, 1999).

SECTION FIVE: THE FUTURE IN THE PRESENT: CONTEMPORARY AFRICAN-AMERICAN THOUGHT, 1975 TO THE PRESENT

Douglas Brinkley, *36 Days: The Complete Chronicle of the 2000 Presidential Election Crisis* (New York: Times Books, 2001).
Patricia Hill Collins, *Black Sexual Politics: African Americans, Gender, and the New Racism* (New York: Routledge, 2006).
Angela Y. Davis, *Are Prisons Obsolete?* (New York: Seven Stories Press, 2003).
Nelson George, *Hip Hop America* (New York: Penguin, 2005).
Steven Hager, *Hip Hop: The Illustrated History of Break Dancing, Rap Music, and Graffiti* (New York: St. Martin's Press, 1984).
Rhoda E. Howard-Hassmann, and Anthony P. Lombardo, *Reparations to Africa* (Philadelphia: University of Pennsylvania Press, 2008).
Gwen Ifill, *The Breakthrough: Politics and Race in the Age of Obama* (New York: Doubleday, 2009).
Van Jones, and Ariane Conrad, *The Green-Collar Economy: How One Solution Can Fix Our Two Biggest Problems* (San Francisco: HarperOne, 2008).
J. Edward Kellough, *Understanding Affirmative Action: Politics, Discrimination, and the Search for Justice* (Washington: Georgetown University Press, 2006).
Marc Mauer, *Race to Incarcerate* (New York: New Press, 2006).

Cherríe Moraga, and Gloria Anzaldua eds., *This Bridge Called My Back: Writings by Radical Women of Color* (Berkeley: Third Woman Press, 2002).

Edward W. Said, and Christopher Hitchens, eds., *Blaming the Victims: Spurious Scholarship and the Palestinian Question* (London: Verso, 1988).

Barbara Smith, *Home Girls: A Black Feminist Anthology* (New Brunswick: Rutgers University Press, 2000).

Karin L. Stanford, *If We Must Die: African American Voices on War and Peace* (Lanham: Rowman & Littlefield, 2008).

Julia Sudbury, ed., *Global Lockdown: Gender, Race and the Rise of the Prison Industrial Complex* (New York: Routledge, 2005).

Jeff C. Young, *Michelle Obama* (Greensboro: Morgan Reynolds, 2009). (juv.)

APPENDIX C

TABLE OF CONTENTS FOR *LET NOBODY TURN US AROUND*

SECTION FOUR: WE SHALL OVERCOME: THE SECOND RECONSTRUCTION, 1954–1975

SECTION FIVE: THE FUTURE IN THE PRESENT: CONTEMPORARY AFRICAN-AMERICAN THOUGHT, 1975 TO THE PRESENT

ABOUT THE AUTHORS

Andrea Queeley is assistant professor of African and African Diaspora Studies and Global and Sociocultural Studies at Florida International University.

Karen G. Williams is adjunct lecturer in the Urban Studies Department at Queens College.